"The Object Lessons series achieves something very close to magic: the books take ordinary—even banal—objects and animate them with a rich history of invention, political struggle, science, and popular mythology. Filled with fascinating details and conveyed in sharp, accessible prose, the books make the everyday world come to life. Be warned: once you've read a few of these, you'll start walking around your house, picking up random objects, and musing aloud: 'I wonder what the story is behind this thing?'"

Steven Johnson, author of *Where Good Ideas Come From* and *How We Got to Now*

"Object Lessons describes themselves as 'short, beautiful books,' and to that, I'll say, amen. ... If you read enough Object Lessons books, you'll fill your head with plenty of trivia to amaze and annoy your friends and loved ones—caution recommended on pontificating on the objects surrounding you. More importantly, though… they inspire us to take a second look at parts of the everyday that we've taken for granted. These are not so much lessons about the objects themselves, but opportunities for self-reflection and storytelling. They remind us that we are surrounded by a wondrous world, as long as we care to look."

John Warner, *The Chicago Tribune*

T0346944

"Besides being beautiful little hand-sized objects themselves, showcasing exceptional writing, the wonder of these books is that they exist at all … Uniformly excellent, engaging, thought-provoking, and informative."

Jennifer Bort Yacovissi, *Washington Independent Review of Books*

"… edifying and entertaining … perfect for slipping in a pocket and pulling out when life is on hold."

Sarah Murdoch, *Toronto Star*

"For my money, Object Lessons is the most consistently interesting nonfiction book series in America."

PopMatters

"Though short, at roughly 25,000 words apiece, these books are anything but slight."

Marina Benjamin, *New Statesman*

"[W]itty, thought-provoking, and poetic … These little books are a page-flipper's dream."

John Timpane, *The Philadelphia Inquirer*

The joy of the series, of reading *Remote Control, Golf Ball, Driver's License, Drone, Silence, Glass, Refrigerator, Hotel,* and *Waste* (more titles are listed as forthcoming) in quick succession, lies in encountering the various turns through which each of their authors has been put by his or her object. As for Benjamin, so for the authors of the series, the object predominates, sits squarely center stage, directs the action. The object decides the genre, the chronology, and the limits of the study. Accordingly, the author has to take her cue from the *thing* she chose or that chose her. The result is a wonderfully uneven series of books, each one a *thing* unto itself."

Julian Yates, *Los Angeles Review of Books*

The Object Lessons series has a beautifully simple premise. Each book or essay centers on a specific object. This can be mundane or unexpected, humorous or politically timely. Whatever the subject, these descriptions reveal the rich worlds hidden under the surface of things."

Christine Ro, *Book Riot*

... a sensibility somewhere between Roland Barthes and Wes Anderson."

Simon Reynolds, author of *Retromania: Pop Culture's Addiction to Its Own Past*

My favourite series of short pop culture books"

Zoomer magazine

OBJECT LESSONS

A book series about the hidden lives of ordinary things.

Series Editors:

Ian Bogost and Christopher Schaberg

In association with

Program
in Public Scholarship

Washington
University in St. Louis

BOOKS IN THE SERIES

Newspaper

MAGGIE MESSITT

BLOOMSBURY ACADEMIC
NEW YORK · LONDON · OXFORD · NEW DELHI · SYDNEY

BLOOMSBURY ACADEMIC
Bloomsbury Publishing Inc
1385 Broadway, New York, NY 10018, USA
50 Bedford Square, London, WC1B 3DP, UK
29 Earlsfort Terrace, Dublin 2, Ireland

BLOOMSBURY, BLOOMSBURY ACADEMIC and the Diana logo are trademarks of
Bloomsbury Publishing Plc

First published in the United States of America 2024

Cover design: Alice Marwick

Bloomsbury Publishing Inc does not have any control over, or responsibility for, any third-
party websites referred to or in this book. All internet addresses given in this book were
correct at the time of going to press. The author and publisher regret any inconvenience
caused if addresses have changed or sites have ceased to exist, but can accept no
responsibility for any such changes.

Whilst every effort has been made to locate copyright holders the publishers would be
grateful to hear from any person(s) not here acknowledged.

Library of Congress Cataloging-in-Publication Data

Names: Messitt, Maggie, author.
Title: Newspaper / Maggie Messitt.
Description: New York : Bloomsbury Academic, 2024. | Includes bibliographical
references and index.
Identifiers: LCCN 2023043296 (print) | LCCN 2023043297 (ebook) | ISBN 9781501392177
(paperback) | ISBN 9781501392184 (ebook) | ISBN 9781501392191 (pdf)
Subjects: LCSH: American newspapers–History–21st century. | South African
newspapers–History–21st century. | Newspaper publishing–United States–History–
21st century. | Newspaper publishing–South Africa–History–21st century. | Press and
politics–United States–History–21st century. | Press and politics–South Africa–History–
21st century. | LCGFT: Essays.
Classification: LCC PN4867.2 .M475 2024 (print) | LCC PN4867.2 (ebook) |
DDC 070–dc23/eng/20231031
LC record available at https://lccn.loc.gov/2023043296
LC ebook record available at https://lccn.loc.gov/2023043297

ISBN: PB: 978-1-5013-9217-7
ePDF: 978-1-5013-9219-1
eBook: 978-1-5013-9218-4

Series: Object Lessons

Typeset by Deanta Global Publishing Services, Chennai, India
Printed and bound in Great Britain.

To find out more about our authors and books visit www.bloomsbury.com and sign up for
our newsletters.

This is not a comprehensive history. Rather, it is a book-length essay that brings together disparate plot points across four hundred years and two nations—the United States and South Africa—as a way of inching you inside a complicated *and not so complicated* story.

1.

Elizabeth Harris Glover landed in the rude wilderness of the colonies a widow. She and Joseph had been married eight years when they boarded the *Jack of London* to Boston in 1638. Joseph was a preacher—a non-conformist preacher—and it was this very non-conformity that drew Elizabeth to him and the two to Massachusetts. They planned. Purchased land. Built a house. Purchased a printing press. Indentured a local locksmith and his printer apprentice son to join them. And then packed up their family for the new world. The journey lasted eight weeks, making their way from Hull across the North Atlantic. It's likely Joseph died of smallpox with its fevers and body aches and progressive rash. They would have placed weighted objects on his body, possibly his own belongings, and shrouded him in sailcloth. But where there is one, there are many in smallpox deaths. So, there might not have been enough sail cloth to spare. It's possible Elizabeth stitched together a patchwork of fabric from his clothing and their linens to prepare him for burial at sea. They slipped Joseph overboard and left him behind in the rocky graveyard of the Atlantic.

Elizabeth arrived in Boston with her two children, three stepchildren, and the colony's first printing press.

2.

Samuel Green was named Cambridge Press printer in 1649. Wowaus,[1] a Nipmuc man later known as "James Printer" to the white men in Cambridge, was named his apprentice. But neither had ever used or possibly even seen a printing press.

At first, Wowaus was a printer's devil. He mixed tubes of ink, fetched type, and pulled paper from the tympan. The hands of the devil are inked black. They're easily spotted outside of a press room. But Wowaus eventually took over the process of typesetting and proofing and had a printer's devil of his own.

Wowaus completed the printing of 2,600 bibles, translated into the Natik-Massachusett[2] language. His name was not included in the imprint, but it was Wowaus who set the type and labored over each page on the printing press. He would have also been the only printer in the room to review the framed type for any errors. Every day, one page after the

---

[1]Wowaus is believed to have worked as a printer from 1649 to 1710, the span of 61 years, nine years of which he printed on the Daye-Glover press. It's unknown when he was born, but one can assume he was quite young when he joined Green. His death is recorded as 1717. In a 1683 letter, Rev. John Eliot writes about the man known to Englishmen as James Printer, "We have but one man viz. the Indian printer that is able to compose the sheets, and correct the press, with understanding." There is no mention of Wowaus in the 1921 book, *Stephen Daye and his Successors.*

[2]Between 1610-1620, 90 percent of the Massachussett people died from smallpox, brought to them by Europeans.

next, Wowaus worked in the print room on the first floor of Harvard's Indian College. The names Samuel Green and Marmaduke Johnson are found on the base of the title page on which it also says "translated into the Indian language" as if there were one universal language instead of the 250 indigenous languages spoken across North America.

3.

Master printer Marmaduke Johnson was sent to the colonies by "the Corporation"—a coalition between Anglicans and Dissenters that supported a range of missionaries aimed at converting indigenous communities to Christianity. He was assigned to work with Samuel Green who'd been printing sermons, pamphlets, and government papers, but wasn't equipped to print the Corporation's order of bibles. With Marmaduke came a new printing press.

Within two years of his arrival, Marmaduke fell in love with Samuel's daughter and the two men were at war. His solution: to start his own press. But until then, Harvard owned the only two presses in the colonies and they wanted to keep it that way. A law was quickly passed, making it illegal for a press to operate outside of Cambridge and requiring licensure of all new presses.

Marmaduke opened the first independent press in the colonies on the corner of Boylston and Winthrop streets in Cambridge. His first printing jobs were religious books for

Reverend John Eliot, followed by *The Indian Grammar Begun: or, An Essay to bring the Indian Language into RULES* in 1666.

4.

Johann Christian Ritter printed government forms and bulletins and tiny almanacs on a small hand printing press. It's not known where the press came from, but it's possible Johann travelled with it from Germany to take up service with the Dutch East India Company as a book binder. It's more likely he ordered the type and press from the Netherlands, awaiting its arrival to the company's outpost, or he bartered for one of the rare printing presses aboard the many long voyage ships that docked in Cape Town.

The company-appointed governor had requested a professional printing press that could handle broadsheets and legislative documents from Holland in one of his regular dispatches in 1793, also naming J.C. Ritter his official printer, but the request was denied. He requested a second time, and it too was denied.

5.

Lady Anne Bernard read newspapers from England sent by ship to Cape Town. With them often came correspondence from friends and family back home with news of their own.

A writer of Scottish nobility, well known across European literary circles, Lady Anne leaned into the gossip pages, as much as she absorbed news of the day. They were filled with the work and social lives of those she knew well and news of the crop failures across Britain, the Napoleonic Wars including the major Battle of the Pyramids in Egypt, George Washington's death, the Russian censorship of Hebrew books, and the Irish Rebellion.

She and her husband were based in the Cape during the first English occupation of the colony, from 1795 to 1802,[3] and she wrote letters daily. In each, she chronicled what she was learning in the papers and what was happening in the Cape, between her home inside the Castle of Good Hope and the country house in the vineyard, for her correspondents across Europe. She wrote of her travels to the Valley of Drakenstein and Simon's Berg. She shared details of an impromptu ball, and she spoke of the production on hospital grounds of Samuel Foote's *Taste*—a comedy taking aim at aristocratic collectors and the antiquities trade— with the military physician playing Lady Bentweazle, a Major playing Carmine, and a General playing Puff, the auctioneer.

She wrote of a slave sale in Hottentot Mountain, a ship that went down in Algoa Bay, and the treatment of the Dutch

---

[3]The Dutch would return to power for only three years, after which the British would formalize the former company outpost as its colony.

by the English. She also took notice of the African-European children across the colony.

"This page is like a newspaper!" she wrote in the close of a letter to the Secretary of State in England to whom she wrote frequently, "That reminds me—the Governor is resolved to have one here."

She chronicled the violent weather and the beauty of Table Mountain fog, how the bachelor governor kept himself busy with evening parties and a group of young women, and the first agricultural meeting. And, of course, the arrival and departure of ships. She wrote of the heat (and how "everybody is annoyed by it") and the governor's beautiful home with its wallpaper and its gardens ("made at great expense"), and of his removal from office.

6.

Publick Occurances all Forreign and Domestick was published in Boston on Thursday, September 25, 1690. It was four pages: three pages of text and one left blank for readers to add their own news and pass it on to the next reader.

Within it, a set of dispatches, one running into the next without headline or space break. A man who'd recently lost his wife committed suicide in the cow-house, found hanging by a rope. The recent sweep of smallpox seemed to have been abated (noting that, overall, it wasn't as bad as the smallpox of twelve years prior). A newly appointed day by the "Christianized Indians" as "Thanksgiving to God" for the abundant harvest, especially corn. And notice of two children having gone missing, alongside the mention of "barbarous Indians" having passed through town. Reports of several fires throughout Boston, one of which took twenty houses and the second took six and a young man's life. But, more notably and concerning (based on the only use of all capital letters throughout the paper): "Another was that the best furnished PRINTING PRESS, of those few we know of in America was lost; a loss not presently to be repaired."

What followed, nearly half the paper, outlined conflicts, ship invasions, military movements, and captures or casualties of the French, English, Indian, and Colonies.

And, like all printed items, it ended with a single line detailing the imprint:[4] *Boston,* Printed by *R. Pierce* for *Benjamin Harris,* at the *London-Coffee-House.*[5] 1690.

Benjamin Harris was a bookseller, coffee seller and printer. He'd emigrated from England in 1683 where he'd

---

[4]This line is called a *colophon.*

[5]European coffee houses made their way to colonial cities. They were a place to gather, have coffee (and eventually, in some, in drinks), to sit by a fire, talk politics, and to stay as long as you'd like. In the colonies, they were also a place where the Revolution brewed. Most sold newspapers and some had printing presses of their own. Harris wasn't the first in Boston; Dorothy Jones opened her coffeehouse "approved of to keepe a house of publique for the selling of coffee and chocholetto" in 1670. Her husband was a minister and rarely home so there was no one around to stop her.

been a printer for a decade. He'd also been imprisoned for this work, convicted of sedition.

Within four days of the first issue of *Publick Occurances*, the colonial government ordered its immediate suspension and for all copies to be destroyed. Going forth, anyone seeking to print a newspaper (or "pamphlet") would need a government-issued license.

7.

In 1696, the official printer for New York printed one issue of the *London Gazette*, per the governor's request. This happened once more in 1698. Within the second was an accounting of the final major battle in the Nine Years' War and the peace in Ryswick. These two issues—albeit foreign reprints of an English paper—were the only newspapers published in New York prior to 1725.

8.

The colonies were without their own newspaper until 1704. News moved from colony to colony by handwritten letter and courier. These were often called "news letters" or "letters of news" (or simply "public occurrences") and read aloud to family and neighbors. When information needed to reach a single community, it was passed from person to person, word of mouth, often originating as a printed post in town square. And, "the General Court would publish its proclamations by crying them out in the streets, to the beat of the drum and sound of the trumpet."

These news letters were also written by postmasters and delivered to public officials as a way to share the needs of each community and news across the colonies. But in 1704 John Campbell published the *Boston News-Letter*.[6] It was printed by Bartholomew Green[7] and only half-sheet a week. Its content was often directly transcribed from the *London Gazette* and John commonly pled for the financial support necessary to publish more. In 1719, William Booker was appointed postmaster of Boston and he launched the *Boston Gazette,* printed by James Franklin and his apprentice brother, Benjamin. A few months later, Andrew Bradford, postmaster of Philadelphia, launched the *American Weekly Mercury.*

---

[6]Within a month of *News-Letter*'s publication, an advertisement by local merchant John Colman selling "Two Negro Men" along with a "Negro Woman and Child" was published on June 5th. This marked the beginning of a seventy-seven-year period in which advertisements for slaves appeared in local Boston newspapers.

[7]The son of Samuel Green, Bartholomew apprenticed under his father at Harvard. He and his siblings would disperse across the colonies to become printers, bookshop keepers, and newspaper editors, leading to generation after generation of the Green family printing enterprise.

9.

Slave traders Alexander Walker and John Robertson ordered their own press from Europe. They were appointed official printers of the Cape Colony in August 1800. They would print all government paperwork and the Cape's first newspaper, *The Cape Town Gazette and African Advertiser*. It started as a two-page broadsheet, printed in English and in Dutch each week.

The governor banned the use of all other printing presses across the colony.

10.

Fifteen-year-old Benjamin Franklin slipped his editorial under the door of the print shop late at night. It was signed Silence Dogood. The print shop crew—including James Franklin, Benjamin's older brother and the printer—discussed and agreed: it should be published. Each week, another editorial would arrive, under the door, just as the first. And one by one they were printed.

On July 9, 1722, across both front-page columns of the *Courant*'s 49th issue, was an editorial signed by Silence Dogood. Its second paragraph reads, "Without freedom of thought, there can be no such thing as wisdom; and no such thing as publick liberty, without freedom of speech; which is the right of every man, as far as by it, he does not hurt or control the right of another: And this is the only check it ought to suffer, and the only bounds it out to know."

The *New-England Courant* was the first rebel organ in America. Its printer and publisher James Franklin was bold and outspoken and commented on the abuses of the times as he saw them. He embraced satire as a weapon to hold the powerful accountable. This was wholly unlike the papers run by postmasters. James enlisted writers to join him. The *Courant* was a collection of voices. Some were his friends. Others were submitted.

James Franklin stood in front of the colonial government, an extension of Britain, and refused to answer their questions. *Who is Silence Dogood?* They insisted on knowing.

The paper was widely read, and James was frequently censured by the provincial government for the content he published.

James was soon arrested and censured by the colonial government. James refused to give up the writer's name. When they called in his apprentice, his younger brother Benjamin, he too refused to give the name.

James was sent to prison for a month. His release papers included a clear order: "James Franklin no longer print the newspaper called the *New England Courant*."

Everyone in the print shop discussed the possibility of changing the paper's name, but James wouldn't have this. Instead, his brother returned as printer, and the paper published under Benjamin Franklin until the time was right for James to safely return.

But nothing changed within the content of the paper and for the next year or two, a battle ensued between the Franklins, Reverends Cotton and Increase Mather, and the General Assembly. The Mathers started publishing direct responses to the *Courant*—calling its writers and print shop "the Hell-Fire Club"—in the *Boston Gazette* each week. And the Assembly continued to censure James and send him to prison for "reflecting on His Majesty's Government and the administration of it in this Province, the Ministry, Churches and College."

An order from the government on July 5th, 1722, required a weekly review of the *Courant* before publication—the first act of content censorship in the colonies.

11.

TO BE SOLD—a cargo of about one hundred and sixty prime slaves. All in good health, just arrived in the Brigestine Lively, Capt. Caird, after passage of 33 days from GAMBIA. Thomas Shirley, Edward Martin.

TO BE SOLD, on board the Ship *Bance Island*, on Tuesday the 6th of May next, at Ashley-Ferry, a choice of cargo of about 250 fine healthy Negroes, just arrived from the Winward & Rice Coast. The utmost care has already been taken, and shall be continued, to keep them free from the least danger of being infected with the smallpox, no boat having been on board, and all other communication with people from Charles-Town prevented. Austin, Laurens, & Appleby.

N.B. Full one half of the above Negroes have had the smallpox, in their own country.

12.

On June 21, 1803, will be sold, at the auction room of Mr. W. Liesching, a slave boy, shoemaker; —he is not parted with on account of any fault—but his master being absent from the colony, has given orders to the effect.

TO BE SOLD at auction:

A slave girl named Alina of the Cape

_____ Silvia of the Cape
_____ Leentje of the Cape
_____ Lea of the Cape, 31
_____ Sainira of the Cape, 8
_____ Catherine from the Cape

A slave boy named Daniel, from Mozambique, a wagon rider

_____ Spadille of Mozambique
_____ Alexander of Bengal
_____ Jacob of the Cape, 11

_____ Solomon of Mozambique, 23
_____ Apollos of Madagascar, 29
_____ Sale of the Cape, 9
_____ Apollos of the Cape, 6

A slave man, a perfect French cook

_____ a very good taylor.
_____ a clever Bullock-Waggon driver, 24
_____ a clever saddler, 28

FOR SALE, a Mozambique slave boy, a complete cook —
Apply to J Jorgens, No 30, Loop Street

13.

In the year 1805 the London Missionary Society sent a press
to Dr. Van der Kemp, but the vessel foundered between Cape
Town and Algoa Bay. The press sits now at the bottom of the sea.

14.

The *Chapman* was the first of 21 ships to bring four thousand
English, Irish, and Scottish settlers to the Cape. They arrived
on March 17th, 1820. More than ninety thousand people had

applied to emigrate, many of whom wrote letters begging for the opportunity to lift their families out of poverty. Some travelled to London to stand on High Street where the authorities would announce the names of those selected to emigrate each day.

The Cape Colony did not have press freedom, but Robert Godlonton boarded the *Chapman* with a press. He intended to start a newspaper. It was confiscated upon arrival at Table Bay.

15.

In the difficult years that followed the American Revolution, the nation's vision turned westward. As territories opened and governments formed, printers and presses (and the type they carried with them) were a necessity. Printing presses moved by wagon and by boat, often down the Ohio River or the Erie Canal, highways to the west.

Whenever a printer leaves a comfortable and "civilized community" and carries press and types "to a point on an unsettled and as yet uncivilized frontier," he is actuated to do so by some very specific motive.

This brought rise to the roaming printer, moving from territory to territory, securing first rights as state printer, starting a newspaper, and then moving on to another contract. Some sold off their paper before moving elsewhere, but many left their apprentice behind as a way to grow a newspaper enterprise.

16.

Section 2 of the Sedition Act of 1798 criminalized any person who "shall write, print, utter or publish" criticism of the government. The following is the most comprehensive list of those indicted over the law's three years:

Alden Spooner of *Spooner's Vermont Journal*
Ann Greenleaf of the New York *Argus*
Benjamin Franklin Bache of Philadelphia's *Aurora*
Benjamin Mayer and Conrad Fahnestock of *Harrisburg Morgenrothe*
Charles Holt of the *New London Bee*
Congressman Matthew Lyon, newspaper publisher in Vermont
Dr. Samuel Shaw of Vermont
Jacob Greenawalt of Pennsylvania
James T. Callender, author of *The Prospect Before Us*
John Daily Burk and James Smith of *Time Piece*
John Vinal of the Boston *Constitutional Telegraphe*
Judah P. Spooner of *Scourge of Aristocracy* and the *Republican Pamphlets*
Langford Herring of Pennsylvania
Lespenard Colie, Luther Baldwin, and Brown Clark of New Jersey
Matthew Lyon, a second time, of *Scourge of Aristocracy*
Morris Llewellyn, James Jackson, George Bartson, Samuel Young, and Archibald Mengis of Pennsylvania

Rev. Jacob Eyerman of Pennsylvania

Thomas Adams, editor of Boston's *Independent Chronicle*

Thomas Cooper of the *Northumberland Gazette*

William Durrell, editor of the *Mount Pleasant Register* in New York

William Duane of Philadelphia's *Aurora*

17.

According to Holmes' *American Annals,* about 200 newspapers were printed in the United States in the year 1801, of which 17 were daily, 7 three times a week, 30 twice a week, and 146 weekly. Newspaper printing had increased three-fold in the span of a decade.

By 1810, according to Thomas' *History of Printing,* 359 papers were in print, 27 of which were daily, 28 were printed twice a week, 15 three times a week, and 279 once a week.

18.

Poet John Fairburn returned to the Cape Colony in 1824 with a guarantee from Britain: press freedom. In just a few years, John and Thomas Pringle would launch the first independent newspaper in the colony: the *South African Commercial Advertiser.* It was anti-slavery and advocated for a multi-racial society.

19.

Elias Boudinot and three others—all leaders of the Cherokee Nation educated at mission schools—started a newspaper in 1828. The *Cherokee Phoenix*. Within a year, The *Cherokee Phoenix and Indians' Advocate*, reflecting the larger audience Elias was seeking. *Tsalagi Tsu-le-hi-sa-u-hi*. The Nation's first paper.

Elias was married to Harriet Gold, a young woman from Connecticut where he'd attended a mission school. Together, they had six children and lived on a compound of their creation in New Echota, the Cherokee Nation's capital on the headwaters of Oostanaula River. This is also where the printing house was built and the cast iron press resided, along with the 85-character tsalagi type.

Elias was named editor of the *Phoenix* by the Nation's government, who'd contributed $1,500 for the purchase of a printing press and type. Samuel Worcester—a missionary—printed it.

Although the intention was to print in equal parts Cherokee and English, the paper was mostly in English, a way to educate white readers on native affairs and to unify Cherokee pre-emptively migrating west as white settlers, especially prospectors in the Georgia gold rush, were pushing against Cherokee borders.

The paper wrote of deaths and births and marriages. It printed the Cherokee Constitution and treaties with the state and federal government. It chronicled Elias' own surveys of native languages and mathematics, and reprinted passages from newspapers across the country covering Cherokee in the West and other tribes.

More than 100 exchange papers reprinted the *Phoenix*, assuring readers across the United States learned about the Cherokee Nation.

And from its first printing, the paper's banner centered a large phoenix, the Egyptian bird that lived 500 years, was consumed by fire, and rose from its own ashes in youthful and stronger form. It published weekly. In between, the printing press was used to publish sermons and other religious texts. Occasionally, they would print legal documents for the Nation.

Elias wrote everything, emphasizing conflicting points of view, including those around the removal of Cherokee from their land. Many of the mission-schooled Cherokee saw removal from their land as inevitable. And it was. But this was a minority point of view. The Indian Removal Act of 1830 legislated away their land rights and required resettlement west of the Mississippi River.

Elias started publishing more pro-removal editorials. Cherokee were fighting the law in court. When the US Supreme Court ruled that the Cherokee Nation was sovereign and the US had no rights to enforce laws in its territory, Chief John Ross forbade Elias to include anything pro-removal within the paper. Elias resigned and an anti-removal editor took his place.

It was published less and less regularly.

President Jackson eventually ignored the Supreme Court's ruling and demanded expulsion. Sent troops. And initiated the Trail of Tears.

The paper's final printing was in May 1834.

It spoke of emigrating Cherokee dying of cholera on the Arkansas River. The whipping and shooting of men digging for gold. The tying of women with ropes, forcing them to emigrate. Details around the resettlement of the Chactaws and Chickasaws west of the Mississippi. And missionaries entering Ojibwa communities in Wisconsin. They note their pause in printing with the intention of returning in July and spoke directly to Cherokee readers in all caps:

"DON'T GIVE UP THE SHIP"

Several attempts were made to revive the *Phoenix*.

When word started to spread that Chief Ross—an opponent of removals happening everywhere east of the Mississippi and south of the Great Lakes—had plans to move the press to Red Clay, Tennessee, the printing house was set on fire.[8]

---

[8]In less than a year Ross and others would be forcibly removed after several Cherokee signed the treaty—not formally representing the Cherokee Nation—and the US Government ratified it. The Georgia government divided Cherokee Nation into 160 portions and sold $4 lottery tickets. The chance to win land.

20.

The national panic of 1837 left John Stephen Wright bankrupt.

One-third of the country's banks closed their doors. Local railroad companies and businesses followed. Agriculture prices fell, particularly cotton which was in oversupply. Unemployment was on the rise, as was hunger. John lost the shop his father had started for him five years earlier and the real estate he'd accumulated on his own: seven thousand acres along the Illinois and Michigan Canal, a dock, and a warehouse.

In the five years since John had moved to Chicago from Massachusetts, he had taken a census of everyone who resided in the town on Garlick Creek—the Yankees, French fur trappers, Native Americans—and printed a lithograph map.

Without his shop or land, John decided to focus on agriculture and education.

One by one, John Stephen Wright started talking to the trustees of the Illinois Agricultural Society. He had a clear message: *We need a newspaper to educate settlers.* He envisioned an apolitical publication that offered farmers a platform to educate one another and to further that education. In this message, he was also pushing back against the political and partisan papers of the time.

The trustees eventually agreed and offered Wright the job as editor. He knew nothing about agriculture and nothing about journalism, but he was given $100 to start and offered a salary of "whatever could be made out of 1000 subscribers." They estimated $300. Any other profits would go back into the paper.

The newspaper was launched in 1841 as the *Union Agriculturalist and Western Prairie Farmer*. It was published weekly.

It was also a place of agricultural study. John opened a warehouse where farmers could study seeds and plants, farm machinery and new inventions. It was for farmers and was filled with writing by its farmer readers.

Its first issue asked in several different ways: *Please, send us your articles.*

As a result, some of its earliest issues read like a patchwork of letters from friends. They were printed just as they were written—as letters with greetings and salutations.

One reader shares his new farmhouse plans and explains exactly why it's reasonable for others to replicate. He has thought about which direction it should be placed and even the plants that would complement its design and orientation to the sun. And, unsurprising for the *Prairie Farmer*, a small blueprint— narrowly printed in one of the page's four columns—is there with measurements, room labels, doorways, and windows.

Another inquires about the best reaper to purchase. And another simply says the "clime" of Illinois is not as suitable as Texas for tobacco, hemp, and silk, so he'll be emigrating south.

It included sections like "The Gleaner": an aggregate of farming news from around the country such as milk sickness caused by Poison Oak in Kentucky, mutton butchery in

Maine, coffee planting in Pennsylvania, mildew around gooseberry roots in Massachusetts, grafting fruit trees and a pig breeding contest in Kentucky, harvesting chestnuts in Detroit, and loo gambling in Virginia whereby the farmer that accumulates "the largest and best pile of manure" wins the pot of cash.

21.

In 1849, the governor of Minnesota put out a call for printers. Cincinnati printers Nathaniel McLean and John P. Owens planned to take this role so, before even travelling from Ohio to the new territory, they printed the first issue of the *Minnesota Register*, dated April 27, 1849, in which they congratulated themselves for introducing the printing press and the first newspaper to the new territory. While one printed, the other procured new equipment to bring with them west.

But James Goodhue, publisher of the *Great County Herald* in Lancaster, saw too much competition in the nearly thirty other newspapers dotting the state of Wisconsin. In the new (and nearby) territory of Minnesota, he saw long-term opportunity. He packed up his press—after only three months of printing the *Herald*—and made his way to St. Paul. There, he campaigned. He emphasized his commitment to stay, whether he secured the official printer's contract or not. He went ahead and gathered advertisements from merchants and subscriptions from residents. And on April 28th, he printed the first issue of *The Pioneer.*

Soon after, James Hughes of Ohio printed the first copy of the *Minnesota Chronicle*. The second issue of the *Minnesota Register* (the first printed on Minnesota soil) was printed on July 14th. And Reverend Alonzo Barnard brought a fourth press[9] into the territory, but he travelled to the northern woods and setup in Cass Lake, where he would print texts in Ojibwe as part of a mission.

The printers of the *Chronicle* and the *Register* were far more likely to be selected by the governor based on politics alone. They both had strong political affiliations which would serve him well. But the newly formed legislature selected Goodhue.

22.

RANAWAY from the subscriber on Tuesday the 30th. A bright colored negro man named ABNER, bought by me of Wm. S. Brown of this city: the said negro is about 21-year-old, 5 feet 7 inches high, or thereabout. Very slim and straight, speaks English only, no scars about him perceptible; had on

---

[9]The Cass Lake press had wrought iron legs and was unusually compact. It was designed to be mobile and used on ships. It's described by the Revered James Perry Schell as "designed for use on shipboard on a trip around the world." This particular press was purchased through funds raised by Oberlin students.

when he went away a blue surtout coat, a fur hat, a pair of cord yellow pantaloons, a pair of brokans, and coarse shirt. The above reward and all reasonable charges will be paid for apprehending and lodging said negro in jail, or returning him to the subscriber in Fouche St., one house from Julie St. No. 43. 20 dollars reward.[10]

RANAWAY, about four months ago, the negro woman named MARY, aged about 26 to 36 years, ordinary size, having lost almost all her front teeth; her under lip is thick and hangs down; she speaks French and English with the same facility; she has small child six months old, which she commonly carries with her. Said negro woman is very intimate with a negro named William, belonging to Mde Gaudin; and both of them have had for a longtime relations with the negro fisherman at the Bayou. A reward of 20 dollars will be given to whoever will bring her back to the subscriber, or lodge her in jail. E. FORSTALL.

RUNAWAY from the subscriber in *Albemarle*, a mulatto slave called SANDY, about 35 years of age, his stature is rather low, inclining to coprulance, and his complexion light; he is a shoemaker by trade, in which he uses his left hand principally, can do coarse carpenters work, and is something of a horse jockey; he is greatly addicted to drink, and when drunk is insolent and disorderly, in his conversation he swears much, and in his behavior is artful and snavish. He

---

[10] The final slave advertisement in *The Boston Gazette* appeared on December 10, 1781.

took with him a white horse, much scarred with traces, of which it is expected he will endeavor to dispose; he also carried his shoemakers' tools and will probably endeavor to get employment that way. Whoever conveys the said slave to me, in *Albemarle*, shall have 40-dollar reward, if taken up with the county, 20. If elsewhere within the colony, 10. THOMAS JEFFERSON.

23.

RANAWAY, in the month of April 1821, a male slave named *Hendrik*, the Property of D. Nel Ls of Bruintjeshoogte, and took with him his wide *Caatjie*, a bastard Hottentot. It is supposed he engages himself as a bastard Hottentot, either by the name of *Andries* or *Piet Hartsenberg*—Whoever commits him to prison, shall be well rewarded. Those harbouring said slave will be prosecuted. Drakenstein—Nov 9, 1822.

RANAWAY, an African slave named *Dante*, (a cook) about 45 years old, short stature, deaf, and formerly belonged to Mr. S. Brink—Any person bringing said slave to the Tronk, shall be rewarded, and those harboring him, will be prosecuted. George Thomas—Sept 6, 1823.

RANAWAY on the 28th of last month, a slave boy named Louis about 6 feet 9 inches high; very much resembles a Hottentot, with a small scar on the left side of his chin, gives himself out to be free—Whoever will apprehend him, and lodge him in any of the prisons, shall receive the above reward. And whoever harbors him will be prosecuted—March 5, 1825.

RANAWAY, the boy *Cornelis*; he was seen on Monday evening last at Pampoen Kraal, and stated that he was going to Mr. Proctor's, to fetch horses. He is about 5 feet 9 inches, stout made, fair complexion, spare whiskers, and has weak eyes. Had on when last seen, a very long jacket. Whoever will lodge him in the Tronk, shall have 10Rds reward; and anybody employing him, will be prosecuted to the utmost rigour of the law. Collision & Co.—May 29, 1828.

24.

INFORMATION WANTED. John Dipper of Williamsburgh is anxious to obtain information of his brother, Daniel Merr, who left Williamsburgh, VA., about 40 years ago, and was heard of as living in Boston within the last 17 years. A person by the name of Cesar Lafayette, of Boston, was well acquainted with Merr. If either of the above-named persons, or any other able to give such information would lodge it at the Liberator office, they would confer a favor on John Dipper who is now in New York, anxious to hear from his brother. (*The Liberator*, April 21, 1832)

INFORMATION WANTED of my two brothers Alex and Willis McPherson, and sister Rosetta McPherson. I left them just below Norfolk, VA., in 1863. They were owned by Betsey Slack. Any information of their whereabouts will be thankfully received by their sister Hester Jane McPherson, 252 Raspberry St., Phila., Pa. NB—Ministers please read in churches. (*The Christian Recorder*, May 14, 1880)

INFORMATION WANTED OF MY SON, Allen Jones. He left me before the war in Mississippi. He wrote me a letter in 1853 in which letter he said that he was sold to the highest bidder, a gentleman in Charleston, S.C. Nancy Jones, his mother, would like to know whereabouts of the above-named person. Any information may be sent to Rev. J.W. Turner, pastor of A.M.E Church, Ottowa, Kansas. (*The Christian Recorder*, May 20, 1886)

INFORMATION WANTED[11] of my mother. Her name is Hannah Green and my father's name was Alpha Green. I left them when a girl; was sold to Joe Pleasant and he took me to Arkansas, and I have never heard of them since. My name is Eliza Wheeler. Pine Bluff, Ark. (*The Christian Recorder*, May 22, 1890)

---

[11]Archivist Margaret Jerido and historian Judith Giesberg have collaborated on a project called "Last Seen," digitizing "information wanted" advertisements in six newspapers where families sought reunification with family members separated by war, slavery, and emancipation. The first ads were transcribed from Philadelphia's *Christian Recorder,* the newspaper of the AME Church, published between 1863 and 1902. The project has now located and transcribed more than 4,500 ads from 275 newspapers.

25.

The US was importing rags from 32 countries for the purposes of making paper. By 1860, only 24 of the country's 555 paper-making plants were in the South. The *New Orleans Bulletin* warned against talk of secession until the south could become independent of Northern ink, types, presses, and paper.

26.

In 1860, there were fourteen newspapers in Grahamstown. Since 2003, there is only one—*Grocott's Mail*, the oldest independent newspaper in South Africa. Its newsroom is staffed entirely by students.

27.

The Song of the Printer

Pick and click
Goes the type in the stick,
As the printer stands at his case;
His eyes glance quick, and his fingers pick
The type at a rapid pace;
And one by one as the letters go,

Words are piled up steady and slow—
Steady and slow,
But still they grow,
And words of fire they soon will glow;
Wonderful words, that without a sound
Traverse the earth to its utmost bound;
Words that shall make
The tyrant quake,
And the fetters of the oppress'd shall break;
Words that can crumble an army's might,
Or tremble its strength in a righteous fight.
Yet the types they look but leaden and dumb.
As he puts them in place with finger and thumb;
But the printer smiles
And his work beguiles
By chanting a song as the letters he piles,
With pick and click
Like the world's chronometer, tick! tick! tick!

O, where is the man with such simple tools
Can govern the world as I?
With a printing press, an iron stick
And a little leaden die,
With paper of white, and ink of black,
I support the Right and the Wrong attack.

Say, where is he, or who may he be,
That can rival the printer's power?

To no monarchs that live the wall doth he gave:
Their sway lasts only an hour;
While the printer still grows, and God only knows
When his might shall cease to tower!

Anon.

28.

Pica
Small Pica
L. Primer
Bourgeois
Brevier
Minion
Nonpareil
Agate
Pearl
Diamond

These are the letter sizes type founders were making by 1860. Archibald Binny and James Ronaldson, English immigrants, opened what is considered the first type foundry in America in 1796. One can only assume type was coming by boat from England and Germany—and printers were using local craftsmen to replace a letter here and there—prior to

Binny packing up his type shop in Edinburgh and reopening in Philadelphia. With him came six font sizes: Brevier, Bourgeois, Long Primer, Small Pica, Pica, and two-line letters. Eventually, the new shop added Pearl, which allowed for 180 lines of text per foot.

But, in 1805, it was Christopher Sower, who opened a type foundry in Baltimore, that pushed for more lines per page. Sower had created the smallest letter size. They called it Diamond. It was smaller than anyone had seen before. And most considered it the smallest type in the world.

Pica would eventually be the most universal. It's used to measure furniture and 83 Pica ems (the measurement of the space an M occupies) is equivalent to 35 centimeters. But it's too large for newsprint.

Minion is commonly used for newspapers and indexes. And everything that followed was part of the race to get smaller. Nonpareil, smaller than Minion, edged toward unreadable, but printers aimed at getting more on the page so it too would eventually become common.

Agate is seen as *the* newspaper font size. It was considered the smallest when it was first created, and it measures at 5.5 points.

As printers standardized, Agates became a measuring system used for what's seen to be the smallest font one can actually read, the setting used for classified ads and market reports and sports statistics. Agate copy gives you between 13 and 14 lines to the vertical inch, depending on who you consult.

29.

In periods of paper shortage, newspapers were printed on wrapping paper, tissue paper, writing paper, ledger paper, and in moments of extreme shortage, they were printed on wallpaper. At least 13 newspapers in Mississippi and Louisiana were known to have printed on wallpaper in the early 1860s.

The *Natchitoches Union*.
The *Opelousas Courier / Le Courrier des Opelousas*.
The *Louisiana Democrat*.
The *Daily Citizen*.
The *Southern Sentinel*.

These four-page papers consolidated their news to one four-columned page. On one side, you might find a purple-red or a pink and cream brocade pattern. On the other, news of the Civil War.

30.

The first issue of the *North Star* was printed on December 3rd, 1847.

The one constant across the seasons in Northern Hemisphere skies is Polaris—the North Star. It's positioned directly above the North Pole and, while the planet rotates and stars seem to rotate with it, Polaris stays almost fixed.

The North Star served as a compass for many slaves escaping north, including Frederick Bailey, who escaped from Maryland in 1838 with the help of Anna Murray.

Born free to manumitted parents, Anna was a domestic worker in Baltimore, a city with more than seventeen thousand freedmen. When Frederick escaped to New York—with borrowed freedman papers, a sailor's uniform sewn by Anna, and a train ticket likely purchased by Anna—she followed him. The North offered both Anna and Frederick a place to work and schools for their children to attend.

Frederick—who took on the surname Douglass after the hero of Walter Scott's *Lady of the Lake*[12]—would go on to work for William Garrison's abolitionist newspaper, *The Liberator,* and travel across the northern states to speak against slavery in churches, assembly rooms, and music halls to white and Black audiences. Frederick was one of many Garrisonians, continuing the work of the newspaper in-person. Garrison published Frederick's first book, *Narrative of the Life of Frederick Douglass,* and almost immediately sent

---

[12]Sir Walter Scott's narrative poem was tremendously influential in the nineteenth century, widely read by school children. Frederick adopted Douglas (with an extra s) from the text, and the Ku Klux Klan adopted the custom of cross burning from the poem's imagery of a fiery cross used to rally the Scottish masses.

him abroad for fear of arrest and return to slavery in rural Maryland.

Frederick's speaking tour in England and Scotland led to a group of English abolitionists making the legal arrangements for his freedom. They negotiated and paid Hugh Auld 150 pounds and secured manumission papers for Frederick in December 1845.

He wouldn't return to the US until 1846, but he did so a free man.

Anna had been left in New Bedford, Massachusetts on her own to care for their home and four small children. She spent only what she made repairing shoes and saved everything Frederick sent home. When he returned, they moved to Rochester, where they actively hosted members of the anti-slavery movement and hid runaway slaves on the Underground Railroad.

Frederick would also start the *North Star*. Its motto: "Right is of no sex—Truth is of no color—God is the Father of us all, and we are brethren." Frederick believed—in conflict with Garrison—that the Black press was a necessity in the anti-slavery movement.

In its first issue, Frederick wrote, "It has long been our anxious wish to see, in this slave-holding, slave-trading, and negro-hating land, a printing-press and paper, permanently established, under the complete control and direction of the immediate victims of slavery and oppression . . . that the man who has *suffered the wrong* is the man to *demand redress,*—

that the man STRUCK is the man to CRY OUT—and that he who has *endured the cruel pangs of Slavery* is the man to *advocate Liberty.*"

Subscriptions were two dollars for the year and advertisements were one dollar. Each issue was four seven-columned pages. Within it, you'd find dispatches from correspondents published in the form of a letter to Douglass and excerpts from other papers with state or Cherokee legislation and slavery-related news from across the country. It listed upcoming anti-slavery lectures, literary notices, death notices, gleanings of news that didn't fit elsewhere, and printed sermons, lectures, and political speeches. On its final page, you'd find an episodic short story (to be continued in the next issue), and advertisements from booksellers, insurance companies, colleges, watchmakers and jewelers, bankers, entertainment houses, hotels (like James Patterson's Free Soil House), the sale of railroad stock, and real estate on the market.

The North Star built a circulation of four thousand, but it struggled financially. Frederick would mortgage their home only one year into printing to keep it alive and any money he made lecturing was poured into the paper. Eventually, he would merge the paper with Gerrit Smith's *Liberty Party Paper* in 1851 and the two would publish under the name *Frederick Douglass' Paper.*

Frederick was the publisher of four newspapers in the span of 35 years. *Douglass' Monthly* celebrated the abolition of slavery in 1862 and reprinted the Emancipation

Proclamation in 1863. He would eventually become part-owner and editor in the *New National Era*, based in DC, where he championed Reconstruction and fought the rise of the Ku Klux Klan.

In 1872, in the middle of the night, their home and barn in Rochester was set on fire.

31.

The Kaffir Express—later named the *Christian Express*—was published at the Lovedale Missionary Institute in November 1870. Its first issue shared a brief history of short-lived mission newspapers elsewhere, before outlining John Stewart's vision of an interdenominational paper with mission contributors around the colony. Even though his language was tempered compared to his counterparts, it also aimed to "civilize."

THE FOURTH ESTATE
(In English only.)

"The newspaper press in England many years ago, received the somewhat peculiar but suggestive name of the Fourth Estate. It was so characterized, because it was supposed, in point of power and influence, to follow immediately after the three great estates of the realm – King or Queen, Lords, and Commons.

No doubt the newspaper press wields a mighty power, not executive, but formative of opinion, as it silently presents the same views, or materials for forming them, before the minds of thousands, or tens of thousands, at the same instant. But this tremendous influence, is neither a miracle or a trick, nor some unexpected phenomenon at which men may wonder, and because of their surprise, refuse to believe.

It is simply the result of a combination of means to a given end. It is brought about by a daily, swift, great and concentrated effort of mental and mechanical activity, in which three of the most potent material forces in the world, steam, electricity, and nervous energy, combine to fill up a broad sheet, and publish widely to the world whatever is transpiring of interest to the individual or to the race—to tell how an Emperor has tumbled into the dust, dragging his empire along with him, —how thousands lie dead, or mutilated and writhing on the field of battle, —and in the next column to mention the price of soap, or of colonial wool and hides."

Isigidimi Sama Xosa, the *Xhosa Messenger*, started as a supplement to the English *Express*. However, it would surpass the *Express* in its power and reach, and eventually publish separately. Stewart would name Elijah Makiwane as *Isigidimi*'s editor, making him the first Black newspaper editor in the colony.

32.

Louis Charles and Jean-Baptiste Roudanez were the sons of a mixed-race Creole mother, Aimée Potens, who'd fled the Saint-Domingue Revolution for the United States. She was among twenty-five thousand refugees brought to the US in the late 1700s from Haiti, the world's most profitable colony, after an island-wide slave revolt. More than four hundred thousand slaves had set fire to homes and plantations. The result: the establishment of the free, Black Republic of Haiti. But many boarded departing boats—plantation owners, taking workers and slaves with them. Aimée was only an infant in the arms of her mother. She was raised on a sugar plantation in Louisiana, where she married and then worked as a midwife, delivering babies into freedom and slavery.

Aimée would eventually raise her children on her own in New Orleans among a large community of *gens de couleur libres*, free people of color, French-speaking and Catholic. She paid for her boys to attend private school and Louis paid his own way to medical school in Paris. He returned to the US to earn a second medical degree at Dartmouth in 1857 before starting a medical practice in New Orleans. He treated patients regardless of race or status.

But Paris had changed him. Inspired by the French and Haitian Revolutions, Louis wanted to start a newspaper and speak of freedom. In 1862, one year into the Civil War, the two brothers and a Creole man by the name of Paul Trevigne started one of the most radical newspapers of the time—*L'Union.* They called for emancipation, recruited Louisiana Native Guards, called for equal pay, and indirectly swayed local politics. It was published in French, hiding its radical content from Confederate soldiers. But it also alienated some of its most important readers— most of Louisiana's Black readers and northerners who weren't literate in French. It was considered elitist. Within two years, Louis rebranded the paper as the *New Orleans Tribune,* also published in French as *La Tribune de la Nouvelle Orleans.*

The bilingual *Tribune* was the first daily Black paper in the country. The federal government noticed. It subsidized the paper with the printing of legal declarations. An organ of the oppressed, the *Tribune* vowed to spare no means in promoting equality for all people of African descent. It actively participated in debate and played a critical role in getting several Black candidates elected to state legislature.

It called for streetcar and bathroom desegregation, emancipation, and the distribution of plantation land to the newly emancipated. It fought for representation in state legislative bodies and integrated schools. It also fought tirelessly against the Black inferiority narrative pushed through its direct competitor, the *Times-Picayune.*

The *Tribune* motto: "The actual liberation from social and political bondage is unity of thought."

33.

All communication from the Ku Klux Klan was delivered to the *Pulaski Citizen* offices via a hole in the wall. First, a piece of paper would appear, describing the print job and requesting an estimate. The printers would respond via that same hole in the wall. The next day, the content for printing and the cash would arrive.

At the time, it was considered illegal, via local law, to print or distribute notices from the KKK. When they were printed, they were often in cypher or embedded in cartoons. Frank O. McCord, the editor of the *Citizen* in Pulaski, Tennessee, was one of six founders of the KKK and the first Grande Cyclops.

Type was set and printing was done in secret. All stitching had to be done by hand in a back room. The job would be bundled up, left outside the door, and disappear in the hands of strangers.

34.

William Bullock of Philadelphia constructed the first machine to print from a continuous roll of paper, referred to as a web.[13]

---

[13]But it's a web of another kind—the digitization of this rolled paper—that one hundred and fifty years later would contribute to the dismantling of printing presses that once occupied newspaper buildings in cities and rural counties.

In 1871, R. Hoe and Co, integrated Bullock's web into their cylinder printing press. It was difficult at first to obtain paper in a roll that was uniform in size and strength. For some, the cost of this paper was prohibitive for the inexpensive newspapers the daily press had long offered.

35.

In 1874, the newspaper *De Zuid-Afrikaan* shifted away from using formal Holland Dutch to writing in Afrikaans, a language with little literature or formal structure.

This coincided with an editorial by teacher Arnold Pannevis titled, "Is Afrikaans actually a language?" Since the first Dutch settled in the Cape, their language evolved, influenced by other European immigrants, the Khoikhoi, and the Malays (Malagasies, Indians, Southeast Asians). Afrikaans children and many adults didn't understand the version of Dutch spoken in Holland—a fact the British used against them in a form of language warfare.

Two generations earlier, in 1822, the British government required English to be spoken in school, used to preach in churches, and throughout printed literature. The goal: assimilation with the British minority. Afrikaans was considered a poor white man's pidgin, not even to be recognized as its own language. It became something people spoke only at home. In an attempt to pacify the ongoing petitions for schools to instruct in their home language, the

British added Holland Dutch as a subject in school. With the aim of preserving identity and language—*the taal*—more than twelve thousand people moved north and east to the interior in *die Groot Trek*—the Great Trek—and established two independent republics.

De Zuid-Afrikaan's guidelines for this language shift: "Write what you speak."

36.

Eight men gathered in Paarl[14] at the home of wine farmer Gideon Malherbe. They were teachers and clerics and farm workers, invited to explore the possibility of translating the Bible into Afrikaans.

They sat in the dining room and discussed.

A few things needed to happen before it made sense to invest in the translation of the Bible, and there needed to be a dramatic shift in respect for the language itself. Their goal was to standardize Afrikaans as a written language and gain its acceptance as a national language.

When they gathered again, a month later, forty others joined them. Together, they officially formed the *Genootskap*

---

[14]On February 11, 1990, Mandela would be released from Victor Verster Correctional Centre in Paarl. He'd been moved from Robbin Island to Paarl in 1987, where he lived inside a house within the walls of the correctional facility. The Khoikhoi who lived here called this place *!hom !nāb/s,* which translates to Tortoise Mountain.

van Regte Afrikaners, the Fellowship of True Afrikaaners. In that second meeting, they started to draft bylaws and a manifesto.

Their first point of order: "publish a monthly newspaper called *Die Afrikaanse Patriot.*"

They elected an editorial team—brothers Stephanus and Daniel du Toit. Malherbe agreed to purchase a printing press and his son Peter would be printer. They would clear out the children's room on the first floor and the newspaper would run out of the house.

They set out to produce a dictionary and a grammar book but, more immediately, they would start a newspaper.

The first issue, printed on an Albion hand press, was published in January 1876. It was sixteen pages.

37.

In August of 1898, Alex Manly, editor of the *Daily Record,* the Black newspaper in Wilmington, North Carolina, and the only Black daily in the country, wrote an editorial that drew national attention.

It spoke to the weaponization of language in speeches and newspapers that implied Black men were rapists and a danger to white women, a direct response to Rebecca Ann Latimer Felton, the wife of a Georgia congressman, and her speech at the agricultural society. The son of a white man and Black mother, Alex pushed in his editorial the need to also rethink *who is raping who* and noted that consensual interracial relationships do take place.

Newspapers as far as San Francisco reprinted Alex's editorial and Rebecca found a platform in many newspapers seeking her follow-up response. This only fueled the campaign across North Carolina to take over Wilmington politics.

Alex had a bodyguard or someone with him for protection at all times. He'd been printing from a storefront downtown, but the building's owner was concerned that the attention Alex was drawing might lead to property damage. So, he moved the *Daily Record*'s printing press to a building next door to St. Luke's Church.

At the time, Wilmington was the largest city in North Carolina and had a slight majority of Black residents. It had a thriving business district and was continuing to grow. Advertisements in newspapers outside of the county and state drew new residents, portraying Wilmington as a post-Civil War mecca, where Black- and white-owned businesses sat side by side and the town was led by professionals of both races: aldermen, doctors, lawyers, seaport workers and business owners. Politically, Wilmington had three Black aldermen and North Carolina had eleven Black state congressmen and four US congressmen.

But things were in motion to change this.

In 1897, a vote by the North Carolina Democratic Party had formed the White Government Union, a secret political society with the aim to install a white supremacist government in the state. It was more organized and operated with greater secrecy than the Ku Klux Klan. Attorney William Barry McCoy, a resident of Wilmington, was elected its executive chair.

Throughout the next year, this Union's message seeped into newspapers, speeches, and rallies. Papers would print cartoons warning readers of what life would be like under "negro rule," including one that depicted the lynching of a Confederate soldier. Pro-white supremacy speeches were happening across the state with a focus on Wilmington. And the rising presence of the Red Shirts—a mounted militia that would eventually merge with the KKK—brought on disruption, intimidation, and violence.

Within days of the November 1898 state congressional elections, white voters of North Carolina vowed to end "this Negro domination" and former US congressman Alfred Waddell called to "choke the Cape Fear with carcasses" if necessary.

Alfred Waddell led a crowd from the Wilmington Light Infantry building down Market Street. As they walked, numbers grew, picking up people along the way. They had guns. And tensions built with each addition. A former Confederate soldier, Alfred positioned everyone in skirmish lines and marched them up Seventh, where they knocked on the door of Alex Manly's print house. With no answer, they went inside, walked around the building, found kerosene, and lit a match. The wooden building went up in flames and the militarized crowd circled to watch. When the Black fire company arrived, they were prevented from stopping the flames until the building and the printing press of the *Daily Record* was mostly consumed.

On November 4, 1898, the *Raleigh News & Observer* reported, "The first Red Shirt parade on horseback ever witnessed in Wilmington electrified the people today. It created enthusiasm among the whites and consternation among the Negroes."

Four days later, on election day, the streets of Wilmington were patrolled by Red Shirts with guns. Black voters stayed home.

The next day, Alfred led 800 white residents to the county courthouse with a copy of their *White Declaration of Independence*. Their message: "We will never again be ruled by men of African origin." Within it outlined a series of resolutions that required immediate action, including the removal of the mayor, and the banning of the *Daily Record* and its editor from town.

On November 10th, someone warned Alex of the crowds marching down Market and then Seventh toward the printing house of the *Daily Record*. He escaped and fled town with his wife. What followed was a massacre that would in fact leave bodies in Cape Fear. The local government was overtaken, and Alfred was named mayor.

38.

Newspapers are the primary record of lynchings across America.

In 1882, the *Chicago Tribune* started a slow daily documentation process of reviewing local and national papers for headlines and mention of these vigilante acts. This is also the same year they'd started to use the word "alleged" alongside the mention of a crime.[15] At the start of the new year, they published their findings: the total number and a list, by month, of name, race, crime for which they were accused, and the location of their death.

The *Tribune* would continue this work for decades. At first, their findings stood alone. Eventually, this was an annual list of loss. Lynchings. War. Legal Executions.

In January 1906, the *Tribune* included a twenty-year tabulation:

"The lynchings reported for 1905 are but 66, the smallest number since 1885. The following table showing the number of lynchings since 1885 will be of use to those studying criminology:

---

[15]Although the *Tribune* was not the first, they were among the earliest major metropolitan papers recognizing the lack of evidence or trial for the claimed crimes of each lynching victim. Black newspapers had already recognized this as fact. The *Chicago Tribune* became known as an abolitionist paper and played a key role in supporting Lincoln's election for President.

1885......184		1896......131	
1886......138		1897......166	
1887......122		1898......127	
1888......142		1899......107	
1889......176		1900......115	
1890......127		1901......135	
1891......192		1902......96	
1892......235		1903......104	
1893......200		1904......87	
1894......190		1905......66	
1895......171			

These are on the record. Many others, if not most, happened in the night, in secret, unspoken, undocumented by newspapers.[16]

39.

Reverend Eiljah Makiwane edited *Isigidimi Sama Xosa* for 8 years before John Tengo Jabavu, a teacher and lay preacher, took over. Under Tengo, there were more than twenty named

---

[16]Books like Molly Walling's *Death in the Delta*—in which secrets are only revealed on her father's deathbed—pull at threads of the unspoken and undocumented many years later.

correspondents covering thirty rural settlements and towns throughout the Cape and Natal. *Isigidimi* was a vehicle to mobilize Black opinion, albeit quietly.

But Tengo wanted more. He was tired of the restraint. He wanted to write stronger opinions and mobilize politically. And so, he departed *Isigidimi* and Lovedale to start his own paper—the first independent Black paper.

The first issue of *Imvo Zabantsundu*, Black Opinion, was printed in November 1884. [17]

40.

The newsroom for the *Memphis Free Speech* was located inside Beale Street Baptist Church. It was first published when Memphis was feeling the exodus of Black families with some money and mobility, west over the Mississippi and north over the Ohio. This greatly diminished the economic base of the city where Reverend Taylor Nightingale led the largest Black church in Tennessee and used his newspaper to push back against the undermining of post-Civil War Reconstruction.

Nightingale was an advocate for self-defense. But across the Mississippi River, in the town of Marion, Arkansas, newspaper editor J.L. Fleming was a peacemaker.

---

[17]*Imvo Zabantsundu* of King William's Town would remain within the Jabavu family, and influence several of its writer-generations, including and especially Tengo's granddaughter Noni Jabavu, until 1940 when it was sold to Bantu Press, publisher of *Bantu World* (eventually, the *World*).

Fleming published the *Marion Headlamp* in Crittenden County, Arkansas. The county had become sixty-seven percent Black after land agents had recruited laborers from across the south to work in the cotton fields of Arkansas. The economy was booming and there was a growing Black middle class of land and business owners. After the passage of the Fifteenth Amendment, this also meant a growing Black electorate and political office holders—from superintendent of schools and county judge to members of the Arkansas General Assembly.

In July of 1888, just months before a critical election, a handful of white landowners claimed they received threatening letters instructing them to leave the county within five days. Seventy-five or fifty or one hundred white men with Winchester rifles gathered eleven of the county's most prominent Black leaders, including twenty-seven-year-old editor J.L. Fleming, and forced them at gun point onto a ferryboat and over the Mississippi River into Memphis.

Fleming's printing press was pushed into Marion Lake.

Nightingale opened his newsroom to Fleming and the two published the *Memphis Free Speech and Headlamp*.

41.

"The newspapers are careless in their statements of crimes committed by Negroes. People read by headlines and when they see the term 'black brute,' they guess at the rest. The press must help in this work. And the press has failed."

—The *Baltimore Afro-American*

42.

"It must be left to the Colored Press to establish truth over such gross and intentional error. It is the duty of the people to seek out and give publicity to the truth," wrote journalist Jesse C. Duke, former editor of the *Herald* in Montgomery, Alabama, in 1893. "Our noble deeds are omitted, and our ignoble crimes grace the pages in double leaded columns. If we cannot affect arrangements with the Associated Press by which we may send out news and correct errors of statements relative to the race, we must seek out and find some other medium through which we can. Let the world have the testimony of the other side."

43.

In November of 1895, the *Indianapolis Freeman* published a drawing that depicted various forms of lynching—shooting, hanging, burning, and dismembering—over a simple caption: "A Song without Words."

In the 1890s Black newspapers published such images as part of the larger strategy to challenge racial discrimination, inequality, and violence.

Black presses published lynching photographs and postcards, redeploying the propaganda of the lynch mob to prove that lynching occurred, and gradually present a visual critique of lynching. Lynching illustrations in the 1890s, created primarily by Black artists and editors, redefined the meaning of lynch mobs and their victims, and laid the groundwork for later forms of visual activism.

In the *Freeman*, the depiction of a Black Gulliver, a gentle giant, being climbed upon and clubbed by twelve white officers and militiamen with sticks and clubs. Off the shoreline, a ship. In the distance on land, three pyramids and a Black man's head instead of the Sphinx.

Beneath, the caption offers an amended Frederick Douglass quote from the *Chicago Evening News*: "The Southern question is a big one however, and something must be done, or the Negroes will become chemists and learn how to manufacture bombs and dynamite, as well as some other people."

This depiction, by whom it's unclear, is captioned, "Still Asleep: Can nothing rouse him?"

Edward E. Cooper had been a journalist and a postal worker before he took over as editor of the *Indianapolis Freeman*, the first Black illustrated newspaper,[18] aimed at depicting "the colored race as it is, and not as it is misrepresented by many of our white contemporaries." The *Freeman* was published on paper meant for books and he

---

[18]The launch of newspapers (or in this case the transition of a traditional paper into an illustrated paper) is in response to gaps or wrongs in the existing landscape. So often, they are in conversation with one another. Cooper's vision for the *Freeman* was in direct response to the *Police Gazette's* illustrated reportage and the ongoing narrative that Black men rape white women—the crime most often used to motivate and support lynching.

worked with artists like Moses L. Tucker, Edward H. Lee, and Henry J. Lewis.[19] It was expensive, but he sought to compete against the best publications in the country. Cooper called it a "Colored *Harper's Weekly*."

The imagery in the *Freeman* made people uncomfortable. Images often emphasized long-standing stereotypes, setting off two years of criticism and disagreement over the visual depiction of Blackness.

The Freeman covered politics and current affairs, but it also covered billiards, prizefighting, bicycling, horse racing, football, and, like most postbellum Black newspapers, baseball. When the Indianapolis Stockings would travel to play in other cities, they would follow and cover the game, and then cover stories important to that city's Black residents.

In 1890, Cooper boasted a circulation of eight thousand, nearly double any other Black paper. But he struggled with the finances.

Cooper paid flat rates for each drawing and maintained rights to each. He leveraged these through sales and rent to other publications. But he had a hard time keeping artists. They felt underpaid and underappreciated.

---

[19]Henry Lewis was blind in one eye and had limited use of his left hand. He was the country's first Black political cartoonist. He chronicled the Mississippi Flood of 1882 and he'd worked as an artist-engraver-journalist for the Smithsonian, *Harper's Weekly*, *Puck*, *Judge*, and *Frank Leslie's Illustrated Newspaper*. But Henry died of pneumonia one year after he was hired as a visual journalist for *Freeman's*.

And he was bleeding money on paper.

After only three years, a wealthy barber by the name of George Knox purchased the *Freeman*. Knox cut costs on paper and artists. And he reused artwork, changing only the captions. But the paper stayed on the issues most important to their readers and continued to visually convey ideas that rubbed against public opinion.

In late November 1898, the image of a burning building surrounded by a mass of white bodies was captioned: "Editor Man[ly] and the office of the *Wilmington Record* destroyed by a mob in North Carolina."

44.

A group of leading white businessmen in Memphis gathered in the Cotton Exchange Building on May 24th, 1892. The subject: the *Free Speech*'s data-gathering and editorial on the common excuse for lynching: raping white women. The *Free Speech* called the rape accusations of five men, out of eight lynched in one week, fiction.

A committee headed to the newspaper's office. Their intention: lynching.[20]

---

[20]Ida B. Wells spoke directly to lynching, in conversation with other papers across Memphis and in real time against vigilante actions, after the lynching of three successful businessmen—friends of Ida's—only two months before a mob would approach *Free Speech* offices with the aim of lynching her.

But, neither J.L. Fleming nor Ida B. Wells, the paper's owners, were found. Fleming had fled town after learning of the meeting. Ida was vacationing in New York. Fleming was warned never to return, and Ida received telegrams threatening bodily harm.

Creditors took over their office and sold it for parts.

A month later, Ida wrote an extensive response to her newspaper's closing and the subject that led to its demise: lynching and white women. "Exile" was published in the *New York Age* and expanded into *Southern Horrors: Lynch Laws in all its Phases*, a pamphlet with an introductory letter by Frederick Douglas. The latter was a patchwork of narratives around Black men in the north, on trial and imprisoned for raping women who would eventually confess to consensual relationships. And men in the south, lynched upon accusations of rape.

This was the third antebellum wave of excused vigilante murder. The first was freedom and wealth. The second was the ballot box and political power. And the third, to protect white women.

Ida calls out the *Daily Commercial* and *Evening Scimitar* for fanning the flames around this narrative, reporting these crimes as pre-meditated and rising. "What is to be done?" they ask their readers. "The Negro as a political factor can be controlled. But neither laws nor lynchings can subdue his lusts. Sooner or later it will force a crisis. We do not know in what form it will come."

Ida would spend the next two years pushing against this narrative in her reporting and anti-lynching speeches across the North, South, and Britain, and Southern white newspapers would depict her as an evil character. While the *Chicago Tribune's* annual lynching data was evidence of Southern horrors, the narratives and details lost in those tabulations led Ida to write the *Red Record: Tabulated Statistics and Alleged Causes of Lynchings in the United States,* an expansion of the *Tribune's* data from 1893.

In a single publication, she gathered names, locations, accused crimes, and she brought stories of victims and families and communities to life. Data and story. She recognized when lynching crossed the Ohio River or the Mississippi into northern states. She detailed the act of lynching, hiding nothing from the reader. She threw a spotlight on those involved, including the newspapers that supported or glorified or remained neutral in its reportage. Hangings—from limbs and telegraph and telephone poles. Immolation in one's home or out in a field. By the end of a club or firing squad. By mutilation. Sometimes by a small group. Often at lynching picnics.

45.

A wooden treadle press was loaded on a train and sent to Glencoe to print special war editions of *De Volkssteem— Voices of the People.* The first was published on October

27th, 1899, just three days after the British were pushed out of Dundee in Natal. The Afrikaaners, referred to as Boers at the time, were defending their two independent republics. The Pro-Boer publication printed with more regularity, often daily and only a single page, for three months.

The *Volksteem* press moved from Glencoe to Ladysmith to Elandslaagte, reporting war developments in the Cape and Natal, informing those on the front and their local readers. Articles were published in Dutch and English and Afrikaans, but not as three translated editions; rather, each article was distinct.

Throughout the Anglo-Boer War, dozens of newspapers printed special editions and several time-limited war-only newspapers came and went. A field press in Natal published three issues of *De Zoutpansche Wachter*. A press in Jagersfontein published the *Clarion* at least twice, entirely in English. The *Vrede Chronicle* was printed in June 1900 before its field press was hidden away on a farm when the Boers escaped the Free State to the Tranvaal. And a printing press was installed in a rail car—referred to as a "flying press"— to publish a government gazette, as the Boers were pushed eastward. Without paper, they printed on ID postcards. Issues were published in Machadorp, in the Veld, in Nelspruit, and eventually in Komatipoort on the border. The flying press was taken by the Portuguese once the Boers crossed into Mozambique.

As the British overtook towns, they also commandeered presses to print their own papers. Newspapers were louder and had wider reach than a flag staked in the ground or a government building occupation.

During the war, twenty-six thousand Boer prisoners of war were held in camps across southern Africa, India, the Bermuda Islands, Sri Lanka, St. Helena, and Portugal. Prisoner newspapers were printed in each. *The Tugella Twaddler. The Struggler. Kamp Kruimels. The Prisoner of War.* And when farms were overtaken, Black farm workers were also taken prisoner.[21]

De Lyddite Bomb was written by hand, three pages in English, three pages in Dutch, by Boer prisoners held on boats anchored at Simon's Bay. In January 1900, the *Bomb* chronicled the escape of prisoners from one of the ships and their recapture. They were moved to a camp on Green Point Common, a sports ground in Cape Town, where another paper was published—the *Skyview Parrot*. Across the country, in a Durban camp, prisoners published the *Tick* from their post office tent. Each issue was stamped by the camp's censor.

The *Barbed Wire* was published to lessen the monotony of one of the largest camps, Diyatawala Camp, built for two thousand five hundred prisoners, but housing five thousand.

---

[21]Londoner and anti-war activist Emily Hobhouse documented the conditions of camps. She was arrested by the British on her return to South Africa in 1901. British war historians estimate twenty-eight thousand Boers—two-thirds of whom were under the age of sixteen—died in concentration camps, and fourteen thousand Black Africans died in separate camps.

It printed war and camp news, advertisements for businesses popping up across huts, and for prisoners to tell their stories. Countless papers came and went: the *Welikade Justice, Boer Afloat, Camp Lyre, Endeavorer, Society of Striving Christians.* The *Diyatawala Dum-Dum* used its pages to also petition for land on which they could farm and to address issues with the latrines. Newspapers would start and stop based on need, affiliation, and entertainment. They also depended on the survival of their publisher. Some were printed on field presses, but most were handwritten on folio sheets and reproduced on a hectographs, a gelatin duplicator similar to the mimeograph.

The *Cossack Post* was written by hand in a ledger with numbered editions, and created by British prisoners of war on De La Rey's farm in western Transvaal. This continued for eleven issues in 1901, even chronicling their release and trek to Cape Town before returning to London.

On the press that was hidden away on a farm in the Free State, the *Little Chimney*—a humorous paper, not for sale, but for tobacco trade—was published on May 22, 1902, just before a peace deal was signed.

46.

Soloman Tshekisho Plaatje—Sol—was a translator for the British and the courts throughout the Siege of Mafikeng, the 217-day battle that started the Anglo-Boer War. He spoke English, German, Dutch, and several southern African languages. He was also a freelance typist for foreign correspondents covering the war.

In 1901, Sol and Silas Molema edited and owned the first Setswana-English newspaper, *Koranta ea Becoana— Newspaper of the People*[22]—first published as a supplement to the *Mafikeng Mail* and then an independent paper of its own.

Sol would edit the paper for five years. It would be the longest he worked on one newspaper or magazine for the rest of his life. His political work—from founding the South African Native National Congress, to speaking out against the Native's Land Act—would take priority. He'd launch two additional papers, but their brief existences reflected Sol's ongoing pull between politics and activism and forging new paths. He'd go on speaking tours or away for political work without return dates, leaving behind his newspaper and family. Issues were just on hiatus. At some point, his wife had to sell the printing press to make ends meet.

---

[22]There was a proliferation of papers after war, representing a concern for the country's future and each faction's conditions and prospects. In 1903, John Dube began his *Ilanga lase Natal* and Walter Rubusana and Alan Soga from East London published the more radical paper *Izwi Labantu*. Sol's first and subsequent papers are considered part of this important wave. In 1909, Dr. Abdulla Abduraham would start the *APO* in Cape Town.

47.

The *Indian Opinion* printed its first issue in Durban in 1903. Less than a year later, the presses and workers moved to a farm, just 24 kilometers outside the city. The farm named Phoenix was 40 hectares. Each had a share in the land. Each grew their own crops. And each shared in the profits, if there were any, of the press. The rhythm of their days was set by the newspaper.

This communal settlement would be home to the *Indian Opinion* for 57 years.

The founders of the *Opinion* were Madanjit Viyavaharik, Mansukhlal Nazar, and Mohandas Ghandi. It wasn't the first Indian paper. Two had come before but were short lived—*Indian World* and the *Colonial Indian News*. Madanjit was in charge of securing a license, selling advertising, and gaining new subscribers. He financed its beginning. Mansukhlal was the *Opinion's* first editor. He would establish assignments, bring them in, and oversee all press workers.

The paper was translated into four languages: English, Hindi, Gujerati, and Tamil. Good translators—who would translate directly into the type case—were difficult to come by and a constant source of stress for the editor. Each letter was placed by hand, one by one.[23]

---

[23]Technological advances in printing were deliberately avoided throughout the *Opinion's* 58 years. Time stood still and manual labor was favored over

At first, thirty-four-year-old Mohandas would write what he was assigned, but it wasn't long before the editorial behind the newspaper came from the lawyer-journalist, based in his Jo'burg law office. Mohandas steered the paper's editorial and also diverted earnings from his successful law practice to keep the paper running.

The *Opinion* printed on Fridays and would reach Jo'burg in two days' time. For so many, the paper was something they heard rather than read. Someone would read the Gujerati section from its first line to last. Others would surround them and listen.

At the center of the *Indian Opinion*'s banner was a map of Africa's east coast and India's southern, tied together by the vast Indian Ocean via which so many entered indentured servitude. At first, Mohandas' goal was to educate white South Africans, to expose them to the plight of Indian immigrants. The paper's tone was moderate. But by 1906, within himself and the paper, he shifted to the idea of the British Indian—one unified Indian population across South Africa—and active resistance.

It's within the *Opinion* that Mohandas formed and explored the concept of *Satyagraha*,[24] the philosophy and practice of non-violent resistance.

---

machines. For the entirety of the *Indian Opinion*'s printing, each letter was handset.

[24]*Satyagraha* would influence Nelson Mandela and Martin Luther King, alike, influencing movements on two continents. Ghandi later commented, "*Satyagraha* would have been impossible without *Indian Opinion*."

The *Opinion* chronicled the life of Indian South Africans and the plight of indentured servitude. Mohandas wrote of labor conditions and the high rate of suicide on the "estates," and protested the policies of registration. It was also a way for news of the colonies to reach India as so many who boarded boats under indentured contract knew nothing of where they were travelling.

The *Opinion* fought against all policies that forced the renewal of indentured servitude. After five-year contracts, a three-pound tax was required to stay in South Africa. Most could not pay for their passage home or their freedom tax. So, they would find themselves tethered to a new five-year contract. The *Opinion* played an important role in curbing these practices.

The *Opinion* also served as a counter to the *Natal Mercury*, often hostile to Indian interests. It also marked Mohandas Gandhi's apprenticeship as a journalist as he would go on to publish three other papers in his lifetime. It had become a powerful vehicle for protest and change. And it had pushed Mohandas into the leadership of a political movement.

In 1909, Mohandas also published *Hind Swaraj*, a manifesto that calls for Indians to rule themselves and embrace both Indian practices and their ability to be self-sustainable. It requires the British to be pushed out of India and for the nation—one Indian nation—to be formed. He calls for the ban of British goods and for Indians to accept exile or imprisonment for this to manifest. He was after *swaraj*—self-governance.

One year later, the printing press on the farm would be used to publish the first edition of that manifesto as a book.

In his final column, printed in Gujarti and English, Mohandas spoke of the recently passed Indian Relief Act of 1914. Within his farewell letter he writes, "The presence of a larger indentured and ex-indentured Indian population in Natal is a grave problem. Compulsory repatriation is a physical and political impossibility, voluntary repatriation by way of granting re[turn] passages and similar inducements will not—as my experience teaches me—be availed of to any appreciable extent. The only real and effective remedy for this great State to adopt is to face responsibility fairly and squarely, to do away with the remnant of the system of indenture, and to level up its part of the population and make sure of it for the general welfare of the Union."

48.

James Mumblehead was printer of the *Oglala Light* for seven years.

A Cherokee man, James was from Almond, North Carolina, along the Little Tennessee River, where he'd worked on a farm and clerked in a grocery store for three or four years before moving to Pennsylvania for school. He'd attended Carlisle Indian School where he focused on music and printing and worked as a band leader in New Cumberland.

The *Oglala Light* was printed in Pine Ridge, North Dakota, in the print shop of the Oglala Indian Boarding School, where children attended academic classes half the day and studied trades the other half. When James took over as printer in 1913, the quality of the next issue's pages was noticeably different from previous issues. And with each issue and year, the paper grew more and more professional. Eventually, James became managing editor, instructor, printer, and was the sole name on the masthead.

Before James, the paper taught students about the trades, US treaties, and the benefits of white assimilation.[25] With James came a shift to covering the community happenings, much like you'd find in any community newspaper, a rolling thread of social gatherings, births, illnesses, deaths, vacations, and visitors. They republished articles from other boarding school newspapers and included news from surrounding towns: Porcupine, White Clay, Wounded Knee, Medicine Root, Corn Creek, and Kyle.

When James married Miss Pearl Johnson, news of this announcement made the community page of the *Harrisburg Telegraph* in Pennsylvania, between Miss Mabel Jones' trip to Atlantic City and word that Mrs. Mary E. Wolf, who had been

---

[25]In the September 1914 issue of *Oglala Light*, coverage of the National Congress of American Indians at Wisconsin University described the event as follows: "Under the leadership of Indians who have attended high positions in modern American life, Indians of all classes, from the tepee dweller to the dweller in marble halls, will meet with their white friends to discuss the destiny of the Indian race." In attendance is "founder of the Indian School System" General R.H. Pratt, also—for the unknowing reader—the man who coined the philosophy "Kill the Indian in him, and save the man," which served as the foundation for all Indian boarding schools across the US, of which Carlisle was the first.

visiting her daughter, had returned home. The *Hot Springs Weekly Star* also noted James and Pearl's marriage was officiated by the Baptist pastor and they were staying at the resort in Hot Springs for a few days before returning to Pine Ridge.

49.

"There are those people in the world who object to agitation, and one cannot wholly blame them. Agitation after all is unpleasant. It means that while you are going on peaceably and joyfully on your way some half-mad person insists upon saying things that you do not like to hear. They may be true, but you do not like to hear them. You would rather wait till some convenient season; or you take up your newspaper and instead of finding pleasant notices about your friends and the present progress of the world, you read of some restless folk who insist on talking about wrong and crime and unpleasant things. It would be much better if we did not have to have agitation; if we had a world where everything was going well and it was unnecessary often to—protest strongly, even wildly, of the evil and the wrong of the universe."

— W.E.B. DuBois, 1907

50.

Robert S. Abbott started the *Chicago Defender* in his landlord's kitchen. He printed his first issue on May 6, 1905.

With only twenty-five cents, he could print three hundred copies.

For five years, Robert was a one-man-show. He wrote stories, selected reprints. He walked door to door, selling subscriptions and advertisements. And he distributed copies to newsstands. He slowly grew and eventually added his first employee in 1910.

The *Defender* could speak directly to racial issues that southern papers could not. Its sensationalistic headlines—a characteristic of the yellow journalism that was selling papers published by Pulitzer and Hearst—and its use of red ink drew readers to Abbott's young paper. Eventually, its use of graphic images built a sense of trust between the *Defender* and its readers. *We're not going to hide anything from you*, it was saying, *just the truth up here.*

White distributors refused to circulate the paper across the South, but the *Defender* was read far beyond Chicago. It was secretly brought South by Black entertainers and Pullman porters and distributed by hand from store to store. Eventually two-thirds of the *Defender's* readers were south of the Mason-Dixon line.

51.

Edward Nathaniel Harleston printed ten copies of a broadsheet newspaper and sold them to his coworkers for five cents. Within its columns, he included several of his own poems and, eventually, to keep people interested, he added news from Pittsburgh's Hill District.

Edward had moved north after a lifetime in Charleston, South Carolina, where he'd been a carpenter, machinist, and co-owner of a funeral home. But, after the death of his wife and some work in Atlantic City, he moved to Pittsburgh, a burgeoning destination for so many moving north.

By 1910, Edwin wanted to expand his small paper. But he didn't have the capital. On the urging of his landlady, he approached members of the Leondi Club, an elite social and literary club in the Hill District. Outside it was unassuming, but inside there was an atrium, a rosewood piano, tapestries and artwork, a library, billiard and card rooms, and a dining room. It was a private club for the city's Black elite.

Five Leondi members formed an investment team for what would become the *Pittsburgh Courier*, the city's first Black weekly. And the team—from business to editorial, many of whom were also investors—had all migrated to Pittsburgh from Southern states.

The newsroom started in the law office of Robert Lee Vann. Without a printing press, the first issues were published in Atlantic City, a process overseen by Edward, and shipped to Pittsburgh. Within two years, the *Courier* would have ten thousand weekly readers. Its distribution channels strategically followed the railway lines and its circulation numbers reflected the growth of Pittsburgh and Chicago, Cleveland and Detroit, leading the *Courier* to the largest circulation for any Black paper in the country.

52.

The poem "Bound for the Promised Land," by M. Ward was published in the *Chicago Defender* and then republished and republished in Black papers across the South. It framed the North as free and safe. It encouraged an exodus—part of a campaign of editorials, comics, poems, and stories. "The Great Northern Drive," declared the *Defender*, starts May 15, 1917.

Tom Amaca was arrested in Savannah, Georgia for having a copy of the poem. Five young men were arrested for reading the poem in a barbershop. The police cited them for inciting a riot in the city and throughout Georgia. Two of the men—J.N. Chisholm and A.P. Walker—were sentenced to a prison farm for thirty days for instigating the poem's reading.

For months to follow, poems and prose—narrating southern horrors and northern possibilities—were printed in newspapers and targeted by the police.

"Northward Bound."
"The Land of Hope."
"Negro Migration."
"The Reason Why."
"Farewell! We're Good and Gone."

53.

Jim Grant, a soldier who returned from the Great War, was hanged in Pope City, Georgia. Walter Elliott was shot and hanged in Louisburg, North Carolina. Eli Cooper was shot to death in a church in Ocmulgee, Georgia, and the church was arsoned because of the congregants' reported plans to rise. Walter Tyler was hanged in Youngsville, North Carolina. Lucius McCarty, a discharged soldier, was burned in Bogalusa, Louisiana.

From its one-room office in the *New York Evening Post* building, the *Crisis*—a magazine edited by W.E.B DuBois and published by the NAACP[26]—documented the rise of lynchings in lists and reprints.

A regular column titled CRIMES contains a list of lynchings recorded since the magazine's last accounting. Locations. Names. Dates. Allegations.

To the right of the list in August 1919, headlines from the *New Orleans States* and the *Jackson Daily News* were curated to fill a single printed page, detailing the slow preparations a single town took to lynch John Hartfield. Three thousand people "flocked" to Ellisville, Mississippi. The police had agreed to hand John over to locals.

On June 26th at 5pm, John Hartfield was burned in public.

---

[26]Although *Crisis* is a magazine, it's important to note that my research discovered a slightly different identity in DuBois' publication: "It will first and foremost be a newspaper: it will record important happenings and movements in the world which bear on the great problem of inter-racial relations, and especially those which affect the Negro-American." It "will be the organ of no clique or party and will avoid personal rancor of all sorts. In the absence of proof to the contrary it will assume honesty of purpose on the part of all men, North and South, white and black." This declaration of identity and intent was published in the first issue of *Crisis* in 1910 and reiterated in the 60th anniversary issue in November 1970.

54.

Sol Plaatje spoke at the Unity Block Club in Chicago in June 1922. He was making his way through Canada and the US on financial fumes. Sol sold copies of his books, wrote for the *Chicago Defender* and Marcus Garvey's *Negro World*, and accepted invitations to speak in New York, Detroit, and eventually Chicago. Ida B. Wells—then Wells Barnett—organized the event. It was publicized in the *Chicago Whip*.

55.

The front of a tabloid cover is like a bullhorn, shouting to passersby.

EXPOSURE
of
12,208
KU KLUX
in MARION COUNTY
INDIANA

In June 1923, a special edition of *Tolerance* printed twenty-seven pages of names and home addresses—a roster of every member of the Klan's "invisible empire" in Indiana's most populous county, exposing the city of Indianapolis and surrounding towns.

Beneath the final names—Arthur Zoeller, Otto Ziegler, and John Zaring—is an illustration of a steamroller headed toward three hooded Klansmen, one of whom is already halfway under the barrel.

This was the work of the American Unity League.

They'd launched *Tolerance* and an editorial crusade against the Klan criticizing virtually every aspect of the organization. But their most powerful weapon was to publish the names of confirmed members.

The effect of the publication of names in *Tolerance* was felt mostly in Chicago. Elsewhere in the state, the Klan was still growing rapidly in 1923.

The public reaction to the Klan in Chicago was hostile. They were staunchly anti-Catholic, yet the population of Chicago included over a million Catholics. Indeed, the number eligible for Klan membership in 1921 was less than fifteen percent of the city's population.

56.

Bundles of the *Weekly News* were loaded into a taxi. Wrapped in mattress ticking, two hundred copies—all they had printed—were transported to the South Postal Annex in Boston. It was March 17, 1927, and the first issue of the paper was on its way to readers across Massachusetts.

Its founder, Francis B. Ierardi, had long dreamt of printing his own paper. Francis was a piano tuner, pianist, cellist and a graduate of the New England Conservatory of Music. But Francis loved the news.

When Francis was twelve, living in New York, he and a friend were playing in a construction site, where they picked up poles and sticks, and started to smash them together, likely an imaginary sword fight. But one of those sticks was dynamite. The explosion destroyed one of his eyes and the other quickly deteriorated. He was left blind.

At Perkins School for the Blind, Francis learned braille, a tool first used for music notation, long before it was used for reading instruction. Francis graduated in 1908, but he stayed with Perkins to continue his musical studies before moving on to the conservatory.

This is when he met Laura Sterling, a kindergarten teacher at Perkins. Laura had immigrated to the US as an adult on her own. The two married in 1916 during the height of World War I.

Laura used to read the newspaper to Francis every evening, something he yearned to do for himself. Francis was fiercely independent. He never used a cane or guide dog, and he used public transportation to get to work. He would carry a briefcase with his initials—FBI—and would joke that this kept people away. His job with the Department of Education's Division of the Blind had him reading brailled documents throughout the day and the Perkin's Brallier & Howe Press had been publishing books for the blind for eighty years. But there was no printed news source available to the blind, and most were reliant on family and friends to read them the news.

Francis set out to print a newspaper in braille in 1918, but it would take nearly a decade until the first issue came off the press. In a building used by Howe Press in South Boston, *Weekly News*, the first braille newspaper in the Western Hemisphere, was printed and collated by volunteers working evenings.[27] Many were graduates of Perkins.

57.

The *benai* shopkeepers of Grey Street in Durban started selling bunny chow early in the morning.

Outside, workers would line up to purchase from takeaway windows.[28] Inside, the makings of curry would have simmered as early as 2am. Ghee, onions, ginger, cloves,

---

[27]The Library of Congress started publishing a Braille edition of the *New York Times* in 1976. Their announcement claims that it was the first "national-circulation newspaper" to be "brailled regularly and distributed nationally to blind readers," but that's not quite right.

[28]Service windows were convenient, but they were also the product of early twentieth-century South Africa, where Black and white and Coloured and Indian could not share the same shops, the same neighborhoods, or the same restaurants. Indentured servitude brought Indians to Durban from which they'd head to work in sugar-cane plantations and railroads. Grey Street (now Dr. Yusuf Dadoo Street) was home to Indian shops, and service windows made it possible for anyone to be served.

and chilies. Masala, turmeric, cinnamon, anise, and bay. Tomatoes, stock, potatoes, and carrots. Beans for the factory workers. Mutton for those with money.

A loaf of bread would hit the cutting board, get sliced in half and propped up on each end. A handful of bread would get pulled from inside and a ladle of curry would fill the edible lunch pail. Hundreds would be made and sold throughout the day. With each order, the curry-filled loaf would be capped by its insides, placed on a sheet of newspaper and wrapped up like a parcel. Old pages of the *Indian Opinion*, the *Pakistan News*, the *Golden City Post*.

One by one, these parcels of news and sustenance would be slipped out the window and carried off to factories, garment halls, and the docks, or carefully eaten along the way, bread and paper protecting the workers from arriving with yellowed hands of turmeric.

58.

Bertram Paver established the Bantu Press in 1932 in Jo'burg. A white farmer, he saw a gap in the market and a way to mold the opinions of the country's majority—a national Black newspaper. He decided to launch it himself. *Bantu World.*

A graduate of Lovedale and sub-editor of the ANC's newspaper *Abantu Batho*, Selope Thema was named its first editor. He'd been a mine recruiter, a teacher, a legal assistant, and a stand in for Sol Plaatje when he was absent overseas.

Influenced by the sermons of Elijah Makiwane, Thema believed modernity was the African answer to overcoming European control. *Bantu World* would reflect this.

In 1944, the newspaper's offices were bombed—twice—by Nazi sympathizers.

The Ossewabrandwag. The Oxwagon Senitels. The OB was an Afrikaans nationalist group, inspired by the Great Trek's centennial. They opposed South Africa's participation in World War II. The *Bantu World*, on the other hand, was publishing a second edition in Cairo for South African soldiers fighting the war.

This also marked the rise of South Africa's "shirt" movement and Radio Zeesen, a Nazi German propaganda station broadcast in short wave in eighteen languages, including Afrikaans. Greyshirts, Blackshirts, Brownshirts. Each were white nationalist groups and each had newspapers. The Greyshirts published *Die Waarheid* (*The Truth*), the Blackshirts published *Ons Reg* (*Our Right*), and the People's Movement published *Terre Blanche* (*White Land*). Each included swastikas in their mastheads.

59.

Ira Harkey was a small-town editor in Pascagoula, Mississippi.

He'd joined the New Orleans *Times-Picayune* in 1940 while he was a student at Tulane and worked his way from a cub reporter to the city room. Harkey went on to serve in the Navy during World War II, and was a mobile correspondent for sixteen months in the Pacific region. In 1949, Ira purchased a weekly paper, the *Pascagoula Chronicle-Star*.

When Ira took over the paper, he wasn't shy. Page four of every issue, directly beneath the masthead, was reserved for Ira's weekly reported editorial. He took on the "reeking dump in the Bayou Casotte area" as a major health concern, "particularly true in view of the spreading polio in Mississippi because of the huge swarms of flies that breed and spread from the open dump."

He wrote of the "death trap" on Highway 90, including bridges between Pascagoula and Gaultier: "a hole five feet long and two feet wide broke completely through, sending one man to the hospital," and there is a "dangerous hump," marked by warning flares.

He also called for equal pay for all teachers: "A teacher is a teacher—whether he is black, green, blue, yellow, fat, tall, skinny or wall-eyed. Teachers of the same training, experience, and responsibilities, regardless of their purely physical characteristics should receive the same recompense."

The *Chronicle-Star* was small, but Ira was up for a big paper fight.

60.

Edythe Eyde typed *Vice Versa* between her tasks as a secretary at RKO studios in Hollywood. It was 1947. She compiled reviews and short stories and editorials. At first, all written by her. Eventually, letters from and reviews by contributors. But she knew no printer would duplicate or distribute the content.

She'd envisioned a publication for queer women.

When she was ready, she stacked a piece of paper—her original—and five pieces of carbon paper together, slipped them in her commercial typewriter at work, and typed the entire publication. Twice.

This led her to twelve copies.

Ultimately, Edythe was looking for connection. "I wanted to meet others like me. I couldn't go down the street saying, 'I'm looking for lesbian friends.' So, this was the only way I could think of to do it," said Edythe.

She never included her name. Although she referred to herself as Lisa Ben, an anagram for lesbian, her name never made it to the page. There was no address for contributors or letters to the editor. Readers were simply instructed to contact the editor.

At first, Edythe distributed her twelve copies through the mail at work and by hand. *Read it and pass it along,* she said. *Please don't throw this away.*

"Don't you know you can get in trouble for mailing this?" a friend warned.

She stayed away from content she believed could be seen as sexual and she avoided politics. Eventually, she avoided the mail. But her short stories explored homophobia, the philosophy of gay separatism, criminalization, same sex marriage, monogamy, and masculine and feminine appearances, and she compiled an ongoing list of movies, plays, songs, and books for her readers.

Under California law, writing and distributing *Vice Versa* was illegal.

Edythe distributed nine issues—a total of 136 pages—of what is now known as the first lesbian newspaper or zine in the country. The tone was light, young even, and far from the tone and language choice she saw inside the news. She estimated each copy passed through twelve readers' hands.

And she was not alone. Lisa Ben had a small roster of writers.

61.

The daughter of Lithuanian Jewish immigrants, Ruth First's career was part activism, part journalism. She was shy and anxious personally, as much as she was confident and focused professionally. Ruth's journalism, over the most critical span of fifteen years, did not represent "detached objectivity," but rather a more honest reportage aimed at the rights of workers and residents of South Africa's growing urban townships.

With the Second World War came a rise in South Africa's urban Black population. Wartime factories and farms needed masses of cheap labor. They came from rural communities, prisons, and foreign recruitment.

Ruth was active politically, as were her parents. As a student, she edited *Youth for a New South Africa,* the Young Communist League's newspaper. Before turning to a career in journalism, Ruth was actively involved in the anti-pass campaign of the African National Congress and the Communist Party, and she was a labor activist in the miners' strike of 1946.

In that same year, the *Passive Resister* launched in response to the lack of protest, boycott, and strike coverage by mainstream media. The Transvaal Indian Congress saw it as a way of bypassing the selection censorship of newspapers and guaranteeing documentation of the country's second Indian Resistance movement. Ruth's writing was published (without byline) regularly in the *Resister*'s pages during its two years of publication.

Ruth reported on the forced-labor of farm workers in the Transvaal, the human cost of South Africa's mines, and other labor conditions. She was considered a radical reporter. She was appointed editor of the *Guardian* until it was banned. Then the *Clarion* until it was banned. Then *New Age* until it was banned.

62.

George Thiem[29] and Roy J Harris spent two weeks poring over the payroll records for 35,000 Illinois state employees, county by county.

George was an editor of the *Chicago Daily News*, and a lone bureau reporter covering farms and the statehouse in southern Illinois. Roy was a reporter for the *St. Louis Post-Dispatch*, based in Springfield to cover statehouse issues important to the St. Louis metropolitan area, divided by the Mississippi River.

An election year, Harris had been focused on Governor Dwight Green's administration. As he reviewed the state auditor's payroll data for the previous year, he recognized some names—those of newspaper editors.

Roy broke the initial story. But, months later, at the urging of a state employee to stay on the story, George and Roy decided to work together to investigate. It took them weeks. One would read names from a list of Illinois newspaper staffers. The other would find the payroll volume for their county and search for their name. The list of editors and staffers on state payroll expanded and contracted, until they had their final list.

---

[29]Before landing at the *Chicago Daily*, George Thiem was editor of *Prairie Farmer* in its 81st year. By then, it was the oldest farming paper in the country and had a circulation of over 160,000—125,000 of which were in the state of Illinois.

The two wrote their April 1949 stories side by side, each at their own typewriters, inside the Leland Hotel room where Harris stayed. Thirty-two newspaper staffers from the southern half of the state had been found on payroll. Some were actually on staff, working two jobs. Most were simply cashing paychecks. The exchange: publishing editorials and articles leaning toward the administration.

Roy and George dictated their stories over the phone and each ran in their respective papers the next afternoon. Throughout May, they'd update their story with new findings, exposing a total of fifty-one editors and $480,000 in payments.[30]

63.

Until the early 1950s, the *Times-Picayune* in New Orleans had a rule that Black people were not to appear in photographs. Editors would cut faces and bodies or airbrush them from existence.

---

[30]For obvious reasons, local papers were hesitant to reprint this story or cover it themselves. Few newsrooms weren't touched by the editors-on-payroll list. Down south, Ira Harkey shared the news with *Pascagoula Chronicle* readers, "Up in Illinois a smelly aftermath of the regime of former Governor Dwight Green, Republican, comes to light through the efforts of two newspapermen."

64.

The Suppression of Communism Act in South Africa prevented newspapers from quoting people who were designated communists (even if many of them were anti-communist). It prevented reporting on groups the government identified as communist and it gave the government the power to shut down publications under their widely constructed umbrella of communism.

65.

At the 84th annual convention of the Mississippi Press Association in 1950, Ira Harkey was invited to speak. He'd owned the *Pascagoula Chronicle-Advertiser* for less than a year.

As he spoke, several newspapermen walked out. All of the service workers stopped to listen, crowded in the back of the room.

And here is what he said:

The basic change at the *Chronicle* has been this: a year ago, the *Chronicle*, like most southern papers, big and little, had scattered through its pages, the word "colored."

John Smith, colored, was arrested . . .
Joe Brown, colored, was fined for speeding . . .

Washington Lincoln, colored, was killed . . .
Four colored men are being held . . .
and so on.

Why the "colored?"
Is it pertinent in this type of story?
No.

We are taught that the well-written news story does not waste words, includes only information that is pertinent to the point of the story. The automatic inclusion of the tag word—colored or Negro—in every story concerning Negroes no matter what the story is, is as ridiculous as doing it also with everyone. How about:

Herold, Jew, was arrested . . .
or James Watson, Polish-American, was charged . . .
or Hiram Cavendish, Irish-English with a bit of French,
    was booked with . . .

As the fact that a man is a Negro is purely physical, and [a] wholly accidental characteristic, how about including some other physical characteristics in our stories? Let's say: James Jones, six feet, one-and-one-half inches tall, weighing one hundred seventy pounds, with red curly hair, medium length eyebrows and brown eyes will be the commencement speaker at Biloxi High School Friday night.

I had thought much along this line during the three years after I left the Navy and was looking for a newspaper in Mississippi or Louisiana. Last July, after my partner and I took an option on the *Chronicle-Advertiser*, the first change I made was to do away with the perpetual, automatic tag "colored" except where it is pertinent. And that, so far, has only been in fugitive descriptions. In such stories, other physical characteristics also become pertinent. But in the majority of the rest, the automatic tag is not only bad journalism, it is an injustice to a people who badly need a bit of help. Treating the Negro like a man does help. And when we help him, we help ourselves.

I wish to say that this is not a "Negro policy." We carry out the same policy in doing away with all tags—such as "veteran held for murder," "ex-GI sought in holdup"—unless pertinent. We do not regard ourselves as pro-Negro. We are pro-people. We are not bleeding hearts, we just don't like undignified treatment for any people, not just Negroes or Jews or fat men.

66.

John H. Sengstacke expanded the *Chicago Defender* into the south in 1951, entering territory long covered by the *World* franchise, owned by the Scotts family from Atlanta. The *Memphis World*, the *Atlanta World*, the *Birmingham World*: these were Southern papers, and they represented the gradualist, anti-agitation politics of southern Black readers. Sengstacke saw the seeds of the Civil Rights movement and an opportunity to expand his staff into the South. They could cover the struggle in real time for his Northern readers and locally for his Southern readers. To do this, he would launch a new edition of paper—the *Tri-State Defender*.

With the next two decades would come Emmett Till. James Earle Chaney. Andrew Goodman. Michael Henry Schwerner. Viola Gregg Liuzzo. Oneal Moore. Vernon Ferdinand Dahmer. Samuel Ephesians Hammond Jr. Delano Herman Middleton. Henry Ezekial Smith.

White newspapers weren't covering the violence, the loss. Black reporters were making their way to the South to report on things first-hand with less restraint than their Southern counterparts. And the *Tri-State Defender* brought the Northern bullhorn to the South.

67.

The *Daily Worker*, a communist paper published in New York, was banned in South Africa in 1954.

68.

In May 1954, the US Supreme Court declared school segregation unconstitutional. That summer in Pascagoula was marked by violence, intimidation, and Ira Harkey's editorials in the *Chronicle*. Just days before school started in

September 1954, the Ku Klux Klan burned six-foot crosses in select locations around Pascagoula, Mississippi:

in front of each Black school,
    in front of the largest Black church,
        and in front of Ira Harkey's home.

"No one not rooted in the South can understand the full terror of a cross burning, this classic threat from the Klan," wrote Harkey in *The Smell of Burning Crosses*. "It is like the voice of doom, the sentence of death, the placing of the victim beyond the pale. Marking him for punishment by some of the most ruthless thugs in the history of mankind. I did not let me wife and children see how profoundly I was shaken." In his column the next week, he wrote, "Ah, Autumn! Falling leaves, the hint of a north breeze stirring in the night, the smell of burning crosses in the air."

69.

"Our free press brings to light corruption, injustice, dishonesty, wrongs of every kind and description in all corners of the world. [. . .] It enables the people to know whether our system of justice is being administered honorably and impartially, as it must be if it is to retain respect and beget obedience. The free press may also be helpful to an accused in dispelling false, distorted or wild charges that would otherwise provoke hasty and irresponsible vigilante action. It may arouse public sympathy and help nullify a 'Scottboro' verdict. It may provide information by which law enforcement agencies may track down and apprehend criminals. Most important, when the press is free from censorship and suppression, it tends to assure the telling of a truth—an eternal bulwark against tyranny and dictatorship."

—Herbert Brownell Jr., US Attorney General (1954)

70.

Alex Wilson,[31] editor of the *Tri-State Defender*, and three other journalists arrived together. It was Monday morning, September 23rd, 1954. The Arkansas National Guard had retreated from their three-week blockade around Little Rock High School, and nine Black students were on their way—the first to integrate after a federal court order.

Moses Newsom of the *Baltimore Afro-American*, freelance photographer Earley Davey, and Jimmy Hicks of the *Amsterdam News* followed Alex as he got out of their car and walked toward the school's entrance. He was six-foot-three and easy for the others to follow, but also too easy for the growing white crowd to see.

---

[31]Alex Wilson's reportage on Emmett Till in 1955 started before Emmett's body was recovered from the Tallahatchie River and continued even weeks after the court case. It marked him and the nation's readers permanently.

Amid heckling, Alex showed his press pass to the police and was directed away from the school and toward a sidewalk. It was then that he was first shoved, losing his hat on the ground.

White photojournalist Will Counts photographed Alex just as he was being kicked down by a white man in the crowd.

Suddenly two men grabbed Earley. They smashed his camera on the sidewalk and kicked him to the ground. Jimmy and Moses were cornered by another group of men who yelled at and kicked them.

A man jumped on Alex's back and put him into a chokehold. Another picked up a brick, but a hand in the crowd held his arm, stopping him. Instead, he kicked Alex in the chest.

Alex steadied himself, picked up his hat, and started to walk away. It was then that he was hit in the head.

Alex was soon named editor of the *Chicago Defender*. He died one year later at the age of 51.

71.

Seventeen-year-old Zubeida "Juby" Mayet wrote a short story framed around South Africa's Immorality Act. A white man falls in love with an Indian woman. They're caught by the police and, before their story is dragged through the courts and in public, he commits suicide. Ruth First and Joe Slovo were running a short story competition for the newspaper *New Age* and selected Juby's story, submitted using a pseudonym, as third or fourth, behind writers like Richard Rive and Alex La Guma.

Ruth called her in. Interviewed Juby in her pigtails and school shoes. And published the story.

"Future Full of Darkness," Juby's first story, was published under the name Sharon Davis.

Davis, for Sammy Davis Junior, whose music Juby loved. And Sharon for the biblical reference to "the rose of Sharon," Sharon being a place where King David's herds and cattle grazed. But, also, the rose of Sharon was considered free from constraint, unlike the flowers kept from the public, inside secret gardens, and also open to the dangers of being plucked and torn apart by man.

72.

Mabel Cetu was on the cover of *Zonk!* in October 1956. The headline: "First African Woman Press Photographer." Throughout the issue, we see Mabel behind her Beatyflex, capturing a funeral procession through the hills of Grahamstown, a local tennis match, the arrival of Reverend Dr. Gow from the United States, and three-time crown Hazel Futa—Miss Port Elizabeth, Miss Eastern Cape, and Miss South Africa.

Mabel was forty-four at the time. She'd been a nurse for twenty-five years in clinics for children and midwifery across the country. Photo editor Benn Lindeque invited Mabel to train with him in Johannesburg. She learned speeds, apertures, flash, and processing in the dark room.

It was an era of street photography and Mabel would work as a photojournalist for the rest of her life. Her images were on the newsprint pages of *Drum*, *Hi-Note*, and *Zonk!*, as well as inside the broadsheets of the *Herald* and *Golden City Post*.

Beyond this issue, Mabel's photography seemed to disappear. Like many others, her work would go uncredited. This could have been gender. It could have been race. Or it could have simply been a way to protect her from the policing of media under Apartheid.

73.

"I was terrified," Juby said. She was shy and inexperienced. The first Malay woman to work as a journalist, Juby was only nineteen. When her *Golden City Post* editor Arthur Maimane shouted across the newsroom with details of her first assignment, Juby inquired whether or not there was someone else he could send.

"If you want to be a fucking reporter, get out there and be a fucking reporter."

And so, she did.

She took the paper on which Arthur had written an address and walked the few blocks from their Jo'burg office on Commercial Street. She stood outside the building and paced back and forth, back and forth. She was terrified.

Juby walked inside and found a half dozen white reporters crowding the hallway outside the apartment door. She wanted to reverse course, but instead she knocked. A white woman with swollen eyes answered the door, looked at the other reporters, looked at Juby, and led her inside.

The woman was being charged for violating the Immorality Act. The couple had two children and they were starting on a legal journey that would last months.

Juby sat across from the woman who started to cry. "If there's any reporter I'd rather talk to, it would be you," she said.

Juby cried. The woman cried. They cried together throughout the interview.

74.

Ruth First was banned in 1960. This made it illegal for her to work in a newsroom for five years, and to publish her work or attend political meetings or to collaborate with other journalists. It also prevented others from using her as a source and any publication from quoting her. It was aimed at making Ruth disappear.

But she couldn't stop.

Ruth was arrested, shortly after Nelson Mandela, Walter Sisulu, and Govan Mbeki, all three of whom would soon be sentenced to life.

Ruth was held in solitary confinement for ninety days. Upon her release, she would be re-arrested, interrogated, and returned to solitary confinement for an additional twenty-seven days.

"When they left me in my own house at last," wrote Ruth, "I was convinced that they would come again."

Ruth went into exile in 1963.

75.

"The power of the press belongs to the woman who owns the press."

— Karla Jay

76.

The Edison Mimeograph fit in a wooden box that you could carry or hide out of sight. In 1889, advertisements claimed its ability to print 3000 copies from one stencil. It didn't require typesetting or skill.

A typewriter.

The mimeograph.

And you are now a printer.[32]

This machine embodies the radical potential for subversion. The ability to communicate under the radar. Edison called it the first electric pen, the at home printing press.[33]

77.

The *Outlaw* was distributed on Mondays in San Quentin State Prison. It was written in secret and was mimeographed on yellow paper. It's not clear how long it had been circulating or if it was a paper that had risen out of that moment, but its January 1968 issues made their way outside the prison and into the hands of editors at a much larger underground paper in the Bay Area.

---

[32]"If the invention of the printing press inaugurated the bourgeois era, the time is at hand for its repeal by the mimeograph, the only fitting, the unobtrusive means of dissemination," wrote German Philosopher Theodor Adorno.

[33]"The pen is a virgin, but the printing press is a whore," wrote Filippo de Strata in the late fifteenth century in his *Polemic Against Printing*. Strata and scribes across the city of Venice felt threatened by the newly introduced printing press. It was less expensive and faster than the hand-written manuscripts they were used to, and gave common folk access to literature and thought.

Within a few days, *Berkeley Barb* published a series of excerpts and summaries of reporting from the *Outlaw*, including a list of needs: "parole reform, better food and living conditions, increased wages for labor, and moving people convicted of sexual offences against children to mental institutions." This drew attention.

Inside, the prison administration swept San Quentin trying to identify who was behind the paper. Eleven men were transferred to other prisons in that process. In a televised appearance, the associate warden James Park said that eight of those men were identified as the *Outlaw*'s editors.

On Monday, February 5th, the *Outlaw* was distributed once again. Within it, was a single line speaking directly to Park: "If you've taken away the editors, then who am I?"

Berkeley Barb continued to amplify news coming out of San Quentin. In its next issue, in large print, it called readers to a day of support and protest: "The walls of San Quentin will begin to rock shortly after dawn next Thursday. Pressure will begin to mount from then both inside and outside the grim penitentiary. Inside, the cons will return en masse to their cells and refuse to obey their routine work orders. Outside, free men will mass to let the cons know the free people support them."

Alongside, they reprinted the *Outlaw*'s detailed list of grievances.

On February 15th, the Grateful Dead played for three hours from the back of a flatbed truck outside San Quentin.

Country Joe & the Fish, Jefferson Airplane, and the Charlatans were also there. Hundreds of sympathizers filled a grassy hill overlooking the San Francisco Bay. And the prison's iron gate, separating the peninsula of hippies and the inmates, had been decorated with flowers. Inside, according to Park, the day was uneventful.

That afternoon, one-fifth of population refused to leave their cells. The next day, that number grew. By the end of the week, up to 2,600 peoples—seventy-five percent of the prison—went on strike.

78.

A network of more than twenty-five coffeehouses, located in military communities, but just off base, provided the necessary space for active-duty GIs, veterans, and community activists to plan protests and publish newspapers—underground newspapers.

Some of this happened organically. It was a moment of anti-war and anti-draft activism, the civil rights movement, and agitation for equal rights generally. But some of this happened with careful coordination, modeled after the radical coffeehouses that already existed in urban centers.

Short Times in Columbia, South Carolina.
Shakeup in Wrightstown, New Jersey.
Left Face in Anniston, Alabama.

New Salute in Baltimore, Maryland.

Fatigue Press in Killeen, Texas.

Eyes Right in Radcliffe, Kentucky.

Ya-Hoh in Yelm, Washington.

Rough Draft in Norfolk, Virginia.

For the most part, these were by and for active-duty servicemen and veterans. And they were often short-lived. People went to war, finished their years of service, or moved to another base.

From what I can tell, *Rough Draft* only published in 1969 and had two issues. It shared plans for peace marches in Atlanta and New York over Easter, an editorial on life in the military, and a series of reports on servicemen punished for their actions.

George Daniels and William Harvey were court-martialed for organizing peaceful gatherings and engaging in conversations with other marines about the conflict between fighting in Vietnam when there are marches for civil rights at home. They were sent to Naval Prison in Portsmouth, New Hampshire.

Howard Levy was convicted for refusing to train medics for Vietnam. Sentenced three-years. Dale Noyd refused to train a student pilot for Vietnam. Sentenced to a year of hard labor. Eighty servicemen had been gathering to discuss the Vietnam War and listen to tapes of Malcolm X. Six faced court martial.

One hundred and fifty GIs refused their orders to Chicago for riot duty during the 1968 Democratic National

Convention. Forty-three were arrested or court martialed and were undergoing trials.

Rough Draft reported on deserters already in or heading toward Canada, and the underground operation in the north, easing soldiers through the legal tangles, procuring documents, finding homes and jobs.

It listed other servicemen newspapers, P.O. boxes where they could subscribe or write for help, and a reminder of AR 361-135: *The right to read and retain commercial publications.* "This is your paper—It cannot be legally taken from you!"

79.

Most daily and weekly newspapers in South Africa passed through the Central News Agency (CNA).[34] At the height of Apartheid's anti-information laws, the chain of liability was long: the reporter, the editor, the publisher, the distributor, the seller. The CNA ran everything they distributed through their own review. Foreign and domestic.

---

[34]When I think of the CNA, I imagine a warehouse of men, hundreds of men, arriving to work each day with black markers and sharpened scissors. Running black lines over and over and over again or carefully excising single quotes and whole articles. One copy at a time. And beneath them, a floor filled with newsprint and book pages, a collage of the voices they didn't want us to hear. And, at the end of each day, after the warehouse has been cleared, a crew comes in to decoupage the floor, creating layers and layers of buried text.

They deleted the illegal and the banned.

When the British weekly *Listener* quoted from Ronald Segal's book *Into Exile*, the CNA deleted these before distribution. When a letter of architect and anti-Apartheid activist Walter Hain was printed in *Life* magazine, it was excised from the eight thousand copies awaiting distribution.

80.

Visual artist Walter Battiss was curious and inexhaustible. In his forties, only a few years after earning his BFA from the University of South Africa, he grew a friendship with Pablo Picasso, twenty years or so his senior, and a great influence on the span and form of his work. He wrote books and articles, founded a periodical, and was an abstract artist who later engaged in performance art.

In the 1970s, he was a member and vice-chairman of the Pasquino Society, a group of librarians, scholars, and artists discussing the impact of censorship and promoting access to literature and the arts. At some point, they also appointed an archivist to collect anti-censorship materials over time. Walter spoke frequently on censorship in lectures and as performance art. With him, he brought "Miss South Africa of the future," a large doll with no eyes, no ears, no mouth, an upholstery belly button because she is meant to be sat on, and scissors for hands.

Eventually, the society disbanded on account of the internal conflict between discussion and action.

And it was around this time when Walter escaped to Fook Island

––a place of tolerance and acceptance and entirely of his own imaginary making. The Island is also his greatest contribution to the conceptual art movement. And, to some, a philosophy. Fook Island had its own language and alphabet, mythology, currency, passports, and stamps. It had its own maps.

Inhabitants of all islands that surround Fook are cannibals.

The Island's newspaper *Fook Nook* brings you inside the stories of creatures and flowers and people on Fook Island. And it recognizes the Fookians living off island in Mauritius, Madagascar, Tonga, Western Samoa, Fiji, Britain, Canada, and the United States. And, in *Fook Nook 5*, we learn that "In Missouri in the United States, a woman has offered to give Fook a piece of land to found a school."

But, throughout his newspaper, Walter shifts his handwritten prose to all caps, reminding the reader that:

NOTHING IS FORCED ON FOOK ISLAND.
FOOK IS THE BETTER PART OF EVERY PERSON.

To avoid the censors, he would write, "This is a work of art, not a newspaper" across its first page for when it passed through Fook Island "Balloon Mail" and entered into the wilderness of the South African postal system.

81.

The FBI's counterintelligence program ran from 1956 to 1971 and made use of newspapers. It focused on five groups: the communist party, the socialist workers party, the Ku Klux Klan, Black nationalist hate groups, and the New Left Movement. Although, not directly, this also included organizations across the civil rights movement. The program was secret and intentionally operated outside the checks and balances of government.[35]

A long list of spying tactics included: "misinformation to disrupt target group activities," and "mailing reprints of controversial newspaper articles [with fake letters] to encourage group disruption." There are also countless examples of when the FBI leaked information, often false information, to local newspapers with the aim of controlling the narrative.

The LA FBI field office placed articles in the *Los Angeles Examiner* and the *Los Angeles Herald Express* in October 1961, targeting the keynote speaker—an MIT professor—in advance of the "freedom of the press" banquet. An editorial ran which claimed the professor was a Marxist and "there is

---

[35] I first read about the FBI's use of local media to plant newspaper articles about Martin Luther King in the *Times-Picayune*'s 1993 admission to their extensive history of racism. Within it, they mention their paper serving as one of six that published false news about King's communist ties, information fed to them by the FBI in 1962.

little difference, if any, between the Nazi-Fascist block then, and the objectives of Marxism today."

On twenty-six separate occasions, the FBI provided information on the Black Panther Party[36] to "friendly" journalists with the aim of printing or broadcasting this information and with the promise that sources would not be revealed.

The FBI also had a long list of teachers as targets. On one occasion, they sent anonymous letters of alert and complaint to local newspapers about a teacher who invited anti-draft speakers to their school.

In 1970, a Tennessee field office leaked "derogatory information" regarding a local Black nationalist group— referred to as "the invaders"—to "a trusted newspaper source." The results: daily articles on the group's activities.

The Newark field office targeted a student newspaper called *Screw* being given away and sold inside Rutgers University's Conklin Hall by "hippie types in unkempt clothes, with wild beards, shoulder-length hair and other examples of nonconformity." This underground student paper became a focus of their New Left investigation.

---

[36]The *Black Panther* started in 1967 as a four-page newsletter for the party and transitioned into a newspaper sold nationally within a year. San Francisco State University student Judy Juanita was editor of the paper in 1969, when two-thirds of the party were women. It was the most widely read Black paper in the United States until 1981, with a weekly circulation of more than three hundred thousand. Its final issue—#537—was published in 1981.

And the Indianapolis field office printed its own newspaper—the *Armageddon News*—to disrupt the New Left (with its own newspaper) on Indiana University's campus. Its first issue was published on September 27, 1968.

82.

The Palo Alto police secured a warrant and entered the *Stanford Daily* offices on Monday, April 12, 1971. They were looking for photographs.

It was a time of demonstrations across campus and the Bay area—against the Vietnam War, the "puppet" Shah of Iran, the treatment of civil rights protestors in Selma, and nuclear weapons. They organized sit-ins in support of civil rights, gay liberation, the woman's movement, farm worker rights, increased admissions to Latino and Native American students, and the Alcatraz Island Occupation. They dotted the city, outside Varig Airlines over theater people who'd been arrested in Brazil and outside city hall during the controversial sentencing of Harvey Milk's assassin. Student groups organized sit-ins and demonstrations regarding issues and social problems that mattered to them.

The newspaper was also often under attack from activist groups who sought the *Daily*'s support. Some would aggressively insist on editorials being published without editorial process. Others would express anger for the *Daily*'s lack of coverage of their issues. And, like so many movements over time, activists grew anxious when images of their activities were published, creating access issues for many journalists. Their fear: documentation is documentation that can be used by newspapers as easily as it can be used by the police.

The *Daily* had clear policies around coverage and images of protests in an era when this had daily relevance:

1) Photographers will be assigned to newsworthy events, and they will remain until explicitly excluded. If they or their equipment are harmed, the *Daily* will press charges through campus and community judicial bodies. However, the *Daily* will not withhold news coverage to force access for its photographers.

2) The *Daily* will print newsworthy photographs regardless of their potential for incrimination. This is essential to full coverage of events.

3) Negatives which may be used to convict protestors will be destroyed. We feel that a line can and should be drawn at this point between journalistic responsibility and cooperation with government authorities in protests that are often directed against the government. Once a story has been printed, pictures taken with it are rarely used again. However, negatives which may never appear in the paper may be used to convict demonstrators.

4) The *Daily* feels no obligation to help the prosecution of students for crimes related to political activity. Our purpose is to gather information for our readers, not for the police files.

The Palo Alto police secured a search warrant for the *Stanford Daily* offices after the newspaper published a special edition documenting a thirty-hour sit-in protesting the firing of a Black hospital janitor and the denial of tenure for a Latino neurosurgeon. Organized by the Black United Front and the Chicago student group MEChA (Movimiento Estudiantil Chicano de Aztlan), the demonstrations turned violent at the arrival of the police. Table legs were broken to make clubs. Two dozen demonstrators were injured. Thirteen officers were injured. Twenty-three were arrested and charged with assault with a deadly weapon, unlawful assembly and failure to disperse. *Daily* photographers were there to capture the scene.

The police did not find what they were looking for: images that could help them charge more participants in the violence.

The paper brought suit against the police—Zurcher v. *Stanford Daily*—claiming the raid was against their first and fourth amendment rights. The district court for Northern California agreed. The Ninth Circuit Court of Appeals also agreed. But the US Supreme Court found in favor of the police.

Newsrooms across the country derided the Supreme Court decision. President Carter pushed Congress to find a legislative solution for the issues. Two years later, Congress would pass the Privacy and Protection Act of 1980, supplementing Fourth Amendment rights and protecting the work product of newsrooms, as well as their sources.

83.

Papers like *Come Out* used movement shops—small print shops with two lives. By day, they printed grocery circulars or community news. By night, they printed underground papers. These print shops in cities like Boston and New York were allies across movements. Straight hippies printing papers for gay liberation, the civil rights movement, the feminist movement, each running through the same presses.

84.

The son of a steel worker in Pittsburgh, John McGoff purchased a radio station with the help of a loan in 1958. He'd eventually come to own or have stake in seven radio stations and seventy small newspapers in Illinois, Indiana, Michigan, and Texas. In 1974, John took a loan of $11 million in an effort to purchase the *Washington Star*—money for which came from a secret five-year-propaganda program out of the South African Department of Information.

When the sale didn't materialize, he offered the *Star* in Johannesburg $26 million for its paper. And, when that transaction failed, he purchased the *Sacramento Union* for $7.75 million, a transaction his South African partners didn't understand. He also purchased a half-stake in the United Press International Television News network—a purchase that interested them more.

Soon after, fertilizer and beer magnate Louis Luyt took a loan from the same program for 12 million rand to start the *Citizen*, an English-language paper launched in October 1976, just a few months after the Soweto Uprising. The loan was routed through a Swiss company and its paperwork marked "top secret". The loan agreement allowed for influence over the *Citizen*'s editorial policy, and stated it was binding and secret, protected under the Official Secrets Act.

Throughout the 1970s, $73 million was funneled from a range of governmental ministries into the Department of Information to be used for this secret propaganda program aimed at "projecting a true image" of South Africa and "countering hostile attacks from abroad." Reporting eventually revealed that it not only contributed funds to the purchase but also ongoing operations of the *Citizen*. One hundred and eighty other projects were supported through the fund.

Despite the many restrictions against newspapers, including the right for the government to close them down, the *Rand Daily Mail* broke this story. These two narratives are just a portion of a much larger, nuanced scandal known as Muldergate, which eventually led to South African President Vorster's resignation.

85.

Students were busy preparing placards. "We are being fed by the crumbs of education," one said. "We are being certified, not educated," said another. They were preparing to march in protest of the poor Bantu education system and the Afrikaans Medium Decree, forcing the use of Afrikaans in schools instead of English or indigenous African languages. For the most part, their placards were simple:

"Abolish Afrikaans!"
"Afrikaans in not a good subject for us"
"To Hell with Afrikaans!"

Sam Nzima and Sophie Tema found the students just outside Naledi High School on the western side of Soweto. Journalists from the *World*—a later iteration of the *Bantu World*, based in Johannesburg—this was their assignment for the day.

Students started to march. Sam with his camera and Sophie with her notebook followed them as they moved away from Naledi to Morris Isaacson High School, a 4.5km walk, to gather more students. Together, led by twenty-year-old Tsietsi Mashinini, they marched to Mofulo Park, another 1.5km for hundreds of students on foot.

Sam moved among the students, ran alongside them, and moved to capture images from ahead of the crowd. Inside the park, he and Sophie watched Tsietsi climb up a tree and announce to the students that "This will be a peaceful march. We are going to Orlando Stadium," he said, "Orlando Stadium is where we are going to meet and prepare our memorandum, which is going to be taken to the Department of Education and the city of Johannesburg."

Thousands of secondary students marched that day, snaking their way from school to school along the dusty streets in song and with their placards. Many chased off younger students who skipped school or snuck away to join the march.

En route, they stopped at Orlando West High School where they found locked gates. Inside, students were taking exams and administrators were refusing to let them leave. Students from outside broke the lock and opened the gates. Test takers started to emerge from their classrooms.

While they were waiting, a young man came running from Orlando East, shouting in Afrikaans. "The police are here," he warned.

Sam looked to the east and could see a convoy of police. He knew this was going to be trouble.

He drifted away from the crowds of students, pulled out his armband identifying him as PRESS, and slipped it on. He did not want to be mistaken for a student.

When they arrived, there were a few vans and a big truck, a *kwela kwela* that could carry prisoners. The man in charge, a white man, emerged from a vehicle with a stick under his arm. He pointed it at students and shouted, "What are you doing here, little ones? I'm giving you three minutes, you must disperse here, failing which, we will shoot you."

Then, the students started to sing the banned song "Nkosi Sikelel' iAfrika".

Sam watched the man pull out his gun and shoot directly into the singing crowd. He didn't shoot on top or to the side, but directly into the crowd.

"Skiet!" he shouted, "shoot!"

Sam ran from where the initial shots rang out, but there didn't seem to be any order or reason to where they were aiming. He returned, still amid the fire, and saw a little boy fall to the ground. And in just a second, an older boy, Mbuyisa Makhubo, picked him up, cradling the boy—Hector Pieterson—in his arms. He and Antoinette Sithole, Hector's sister, started running.

Sam captured this, the first of six images from what he describes as "under the line of bullets." Sophie opened the press car door and directed them in. Their driver took Hector, his sister, and Mbuyisa to the clinic.

Sam quickly rewound his half-used roll of film, removed it from his camera, and slipped it in his sock.

86.

"What the eye doesn't see the mind doesn't know, and the heart will not grieve over."

— Bishop Desmond Tutu

87.

World editor Percy Qoboza did not want to use Sam's photographs. There was a big debate in the newsroom. Percy was concerned the image would spark civil war. Word of Hector's death had already spread, and Soweto was uprising.

One of those images was sent over the wire and published in the *World*[37] the next day. Hector Pieterson was seen across Europe and Asia and the Americas. It was printed and shared across Soweto. It was inside people's homes.

It would become the first photograph banned by the government and the image that would push Sam into exile.

88.

Most South African newspapers had a "resident government spy"—an undercover worker from the Bureau of State Security. Everyone knew who their BOSS agent was.

The paper's first edition would be headed out and the phone would ring. The Magistrate's office was calling to put an injunction on a particular story and you'd be calling back trucks with one hundred thousand copies on their way to distribution sites. They'd all have to be dumped. The story

---

[37]The *World* would be banned in 1977.

would be replaced with another, and the paper would go to print again.

89.

Donald Woods would reserve his most outspoken editorials for Fridays. Most of the government ministers had farms they would go to for the weekend and that would give them two days to cool down before returning to their offices and deciding to respond. Under Woods' editorship, none of the *Daily Dispatch* journalists in East London were jailed for what they wrote.

But in 1977, Donald investigated the death of Steve Biko.

He was banned from working in a newsroom, from publicly speaking or being quoted in print. The security police wired Woods' house with surveillance microphones and recorded all telephone calls. Twice, officers fired bullets into their home. His wife Wendy was an active member of Black Sash, a campaign against the imprisonment of political detainees, but Donald's banning brought even greater attention to their home.

Wendy arranged to attend the thirteen-day Biko inquest in Pretoria and, while she was away, their five-year-old daughter received a parcel in the mail. Security police had laced a t-shirt with acid-powder and shipped it to their home—burning her face and arms.

David and his family went into exile.

90.

In its seventh year, the pages of *New Directions for Women* reflected the second wave feminist movement and the push to pass the Equal Rights Amendment (ERA). Women choosing sterilization. The fight for equity in sports. The right to quality and compassionate healthcare and services to battered women and victims of rape. The war against birth control and equal access to abortion. The rise of Rural American Women (RAW) as a political voice. The post-Roe backlash in the 1978 elections against pro-choice politicians. And two thousand women, mostly nuns, "parading"[38] at the Catholic Women's Conference for the right to be ordained.

It'd only been a year since the gathering of nearly twenty thousand women delegates and attendees for the National Women's Conference, an initiative funded by Congress and organized by the National Commission on the Observance of International Women's Year. Lady Bird Johnson, Betty Ford, and Rosalynn Carter—direct connections to the White House—set the tone and defined the power and seriousness of the event.

The Catholic contingency was divided: laywomen considered themselves pro-family and therefore most were against the ERA, claiming existing protections for women were enough, but nuns were pro ERA, seeing this as the path

---

[38]We wouldn't dare protest. We're *parading*!

necessary for growth in the church and the opportunity for women to be ordained as deacons and priests.

New Directions for Women began as a mimeographed newsletter in 1972 in New Jersey, but it quickly became a tabloid-size quarterly newspaper, and the first feminist newspaper in the state and nation. Edited by Paula Kassell, a member of the of the National Organization for Women (NOW), the paper filled a need for no-nonsense reportage from a feminist perspective. It ran state, national, and international news stories, book reviews, women's history articles, and editorials.

91.

On the page, Juby was Sharon Davis. And sometimes Betty Human (a column for the *Golden City Post*). And sometimes Dolly (for the Dear Dolly column in *Drum*). And sometimes Pat Baker (for a cookery column). And Sometimes Gammatjie (for which Juby made selections from submitted jokes and curated the "Gammatjie's Jokes" column).

When given the space, Juby wrote about equity, gender, and race. She continued to report on the Immorality Act and the people impacted by the law criminalizing "sex between whites and all non-whites." Like she had done in her first short story, published as a teenager, Juby would openly criticize the policies of Apartheid through reportage and short stories.

Juby was raised just outside of Johannesburg in Fietas, a small vibrant community where Malay, Indian, Coloured, and some poor white families peacefully coexisted. Fourteenth Street in the Pageview area of Fietas was lined with bargain tables and traders on the pavement, just outside businesses whose shopkeepers lived upstairs. Shoppers were from across Jo'burg and represented the whole of South Africa.

But everything changed after 1969. Residents were notified of relocation plans based on their racial classification – the foundation of all Apartheid laws. Indians were sent to Lenasia. Malays and Coloureds were sent to Eldorado Park. The process would span ten years.

But, unlike other forced removals, where buildings were just bulldozed, Fietas residents fought to keep some spaces. Two mosques on Fifteenth and Twenty-fifth Streets, and the Anglican Church on Krause Road, the latter of which was used as a refuge throughout the Soweto uprising in 1976, and, during the evictions, its yard was filled with tents to house the homeless. Eventually, people who owned land were forced to sell to the government.

Fietas and its razing not only influenced Juby's work, but also her identity. Juby's resistance expanded from the page to the street.

In 1973, Juby was a founding member of the Union for Black Journalists. Their motto: to tell the truth. They held regular meetings and published their own paper, the *Bulletin*.

Joe Thloloe, Zwelakhe Sisulu, Phil Mtimkulu. Sam Nzima. They were all actively publishing within the Union's pages.

The paper contained some revealing articles about the activities of the South African Police during the Soweto uprisings. It was banned along with the Union in 1977. The Soweto Uprising had tightened the government's grip on media. Black journalists were the target.

But they simply formed a new organization—the Writers Association of South Africa. As a precaution, Juby and Phil withdrew what the Union had in its bank account. And within days, the police confiscated the funds and arrested them for theft.

She was acquitted and then quickly arrested once again. This time, four UBJ officials—Juby, Joe, Mike Nkadimeng and Mike Norton—were charged for producing an undesirable publication.

Juby would spend five months in the Number Four Prison.

"In there," she said, "we fomented our own kind of trouble. They can lock you up, but they can't lock your mind up. Your mind is forever free."

92.

In 1982, the South African government purchased twelve ads in the *Wall Street Journal*. Each cost $24,000. A similar series was purchased in the *Washington Post*. Each cost more than $5,200. In each was imagery of an integrated South Africa, one with professional and social equity—"the changing face" of the nation. This was three years into the US ban on exporting goods to South Africa.

That same year, Ruth First was killed by a letter bomb sent to her by the South African security police. She'd been going through her mail in her office at the University in Maputo.

93.

The first six issues of *Link/Skeykl* were cut and paste (and sometimes stapled) and then copied at a local print shop. Within months of forming GASA—the Gay Association of South Africa—Henk Botha and Alex Robbertze found themselves in charge of the monthly newsletter. For twenty-four Rand a year, you could secure membership and receive news in the mail.

It was 1982.

Those first few months chronicled the formation of local chapters, GASA's constitution and mission statement, film and theater reviews, and updates on fundraisers and events. They were even opening a storefront office. Growth is clearest in the telephone directory with contacts for the discussion and drama groups, Gay Day organizing, the gay history project, hiking and motorcycle clubs, the married gay group and religious fellowships, *Link/Skeykl,* and *Pink Pages.*

Within its pages are also columns addressing anxiety around the possible tampering of *Link/Skeykl* in the mail, a series on "you and the law," outlining and discussing the common law and statutes that criminalize being gay in South Africa, and the recent murder of a member.

After the Immorality Act of 1956 and the Forest Town Raid of 1966, there was a spark of a movement but not even an underground movement. It was three steps below underground.

In 1980, the raid on New Mandy's in downtown Jo'burg ignited what some considered South Africa's gay liberation movement. Small groups started to form across the country—mostly white, male, and middle class. In 1981, twenty-four members from across three groups—Lambda, Alternative Men's Organization (AMO), and Unite—decided to merge with the aim of establishing the first national gay organization in the country.

After six issues of the newsletter, Henk decided they were ready to start printing *Link/Skeykl* as a tabloid, members-only newspaper. He wanted to see more space and color images, to professionalize their news. Membership had climbed to nearly three thousand in less than a year, but no one wanted to see their image in the paper and no one wanted their name in print. Many bylines remained first names only, like Michael, the in-house lawyer. But they continued to receive letters of congratulations, queries, offers to volunteer and, "thank goodness, no letter bombs."

They would publish thirty-seven issues.

94.

"White members of the public will suffer more by the blackout of news, because the blacks live in township where the revolution is occurring. They know by sight and word of mouth what is occurring, but the whites in their secure white suburbs do not."

—Percy Qoboza

95.

"We must be visible if we are going to be liberated."

—Simon Nkoli

96.

In a zip car and hoodie, Alexandra Bell made her way through Brooklyn wheat pasting two pages of the *New York Times* on the side of buildings and on the walls of subway stations. It was New Year's Eve 2016.

This was her first installment of *Counternarratives*.

Earlier that year, a spate of police shootings that drew wider media attention also drew Alexandra and her friends to gather after each.

In July, the day Alton Sterling was killed in Louisiana, they gathered in Brooklyn. Closed the bar. And returned to their respective homes around the city.

The next day, Philando Castile was killed in Minnesota.

The crowdsourcing of content across friends via text pulled their range of media consumption into one space. Headline after headline.

A month later, Korryn Gaines was killed in Maryland.

"She'd been shot and killed by cops in her home in Baltimore," said Bell, "And I read a headline and the headline said she was cradling her kid and a gun. But it never said she was in her own home. That was missing from the headline. And that felt important to me."

And that is when Alexandra could crystalize what was bothering her four years earlier, as a journalism graduate student reading three papers a day examining how coverage differed from one paper to the next, specifically around the time of Trayvon Martin's death.

"There's a way that sometimes news publications publish the facts but in ways that don't feel true."

Alexandra then established a process to tease that out.

At first, she took the *NYT* front page with side-by-side narratives chronicling Ferguson. Officer Darren Wilson on the left. Teenager Michael Brown on the right. At quick glance, one could see this as equitable and fair. But Alexandra didn't see this. She started to cross out the words that felt untrue or contextually manipulative or distracting. She weighed what it means to be fair and equitable between the narratives of a kid and a cop, and what the equity on the page—thirty-eight lines, side by side, photo placement and size—actually implies to the reader. "Equal culpability," said Bell, "and I don't believe that to be true." She continued to cross out lines. What remained was thin. The bare facts.

Crossroads in Ferguson

On the left, "Officer Darren Wilson fatally shot an unarmed Black teenager Michael Brown." On the right, "A teenager with Promise. Michael Brown Jr., his shooting death by Darren Wilson, a white police officer."

Alexandra kept the *Times* masthead but eliminated the rest of A1. She enlarged the two crossed out columns, creating a new version of the front page.

She countered the information in the article that ended up under black lines—"they talked about him rapping and cursing and doing drugs"—with an image that captured Michael as the young man with promise.

And with this, she created a second page. The same masthead. The new headline, "A Teenager with Promise," over a very large image of Michael Brown in his graduation photo. Cap and gown.

Alexandra printed copies of the two pages (two feet by three feet) and, at 2am with a less than perfect wheat paste in hand, started to hang them on the sides of buildings around Brooklyn. Eye height.

Some were torn down. Some blew away (because the "wheat paste recipe at the time was trash"). But, on one particular wall, people were reading. People were talking. Then, someone covered it up with something larger. And some social media anger about the coverup caused people to tear down the larger work, and reveal once again the two pages.

In time, the pages started to wear away, and the wall, filled with graffiti and other art, was ordered to be painted. But whoever was tasked with that job painted over nearly everything, leaving "A Teenager with Promise" and the majority of Michael Brown's photo visible.

Alexandra's work[39] got larger (from 2x3 feet to 6x9 feet to 5x20 feet). And more complex, building counternarratives with newspapers from around the country. She started to annotate and show her work, creating a procedural narrative or panel essay on the sides of buildings.

Illegal at first, unsigned, watching the engagement around and impact of her work from the side. Quickly, pasted with permission. And then, by invitation.

97.

David Steward, the official spokesman for South Africa's new Government Bureau of Information, ran "school for the

---

[39]Alexandra identifies as an interdisciplinary artist. I see her as an investigative reporter who translates this work and incites both thought and hopefully action into visual art across mediums and form.

press" every day in a manner reminiscent of the "Five o'clock follies" run by the US Army for the press in Vietnam.

You could go along to a daily briefing in Pretoria at 5pm and be told what had happened around the country. You could submit questions, but no reporting of any unrest was publishable unless it was submitted to the Bureau and the Bureau then gave you the authorized version of whether it was true or not true.

The object of this exercise was to substitute eye-witness reporting with the government's version. *What you saw did not happen if the Bureau said otherwise.*

98.

Through a school board meeting, boycotting students were warned by the police: *return to school by Wednesday or you'll be shot.* They responded with a list of grievances. Within hours of the meeting's end, the street lights in Zweletemba went dark and the beer hall, WCBD office, local Councellor's home, and a garbage truck were on fire. On Wednesday, the students returned to school. The police taunted them and fired tear-gas into the school yard. Children and adults were arrested and jailed.

But this was not covered in local or national newspapers. It was detailed by witnesses and chronicled in the first issue of *Crisis News*.

"This bulletin is the first in a series of pamphlets that attempt to tell the truth of what is happening in our country," explained the first issue. "It will be told through the words of those from emergency areas, and by those who have visited these areas to collect information." Its launch in September 1985 coincided with emergencies in thirty-six areas.

The first four-page, typed issue was produced in direct response to reporting blackouts. It documents three incidents: the funeral of the Cradock Four, a week-long school boycott, and the attack of mourners[40] during the funeral procession for Thembile Mathiso, killed by the police in a student march.

The Western Province Council of Churches—an interdenominational forum and anti-Apartheid organization—published thirty-two issues over four years.

---

[40]Before the funeral, police dropped pamphlets from the air, outlining restrictions: no political speeches, no banners, the procession should follow the shortest route, and all mourners must be away from the area by 3pm. As the nearly six thousand mourners were moving from the cemetery to Thembile's home to wash their hands—an essential final step in a traditional funeral—the police fired rubber bullets and tear gas at the mourners to force them to disperse. Mourners who did not move were chased and beaten with rifle butts and batons.

They'd chronicle township curfews, bans, peaceful protests, security actions, groups acting with indemnity, shootings and injuries, those suffering, and moments and individuals that give hope.

But what started as a response to a moment of crisis slowly evolved into regular news.

At the base of its second page, *Crisis* speaks directly to the reader: "A commitment to justice means being aware of injustice. Read this bulletin and show it to your friends."

99.

Max du Preez, the editor of the only anti-Apartheid paper published in Afrikaans, was given six months jail time and five years suspension for quoting one of the 543 "listed" people deemed not to be quoted.

100.

"The emerging new press has taken the lead and are reporting on the events within black communities and the black townships. The problem now is when the government expected the voices of dissent to be silenced, as they had been in the previous three decades, the voices in fact have been intensified," Ameen Akjalwaya[41] testified in front of the U.S. Congressional Committee on Foreign Affairs.

"The irony is that those people—politicians as well as journalists in South Africa—who propagate the idea of a genuine democracy, a genuine non-racial or anti-racist democracy—are being criminalized. Our belief is that, if we are to be criminalized and regarded as criminals because we try to enforce a decent human system in our own country, then we are proud to be criminals."

101.

"There is a particular damage that press censorship has in a society like South Africa. It is indeed true that there are many other countries in the world where there is censorship, there are many other countries in the world where there's

---

[41]Ameen studied medicine overseas and returned to South Africa to work in journalism. He lived in Lenasia, a product of the Group Areas Act and a township for Indians. In 1978, he was appointed political reporter for the *Rand Daily Mail*, the first Black person to earn such a position within a white newspaper's staff. *This a South African sense of Blackness that has evolved over time. A Blackness that is more about defining a collective oppressed than it is a specific racial categorization, like the constructs of Apartheid.* After the closure of the *Daily Mail* and the *Sunday Express,* Ameen founded the *Indicator,* one of the "alternative press" that escalated the Apartheid government's censorship efforts and aggression toward the media throughout the 80s. In 1985 it had a circulation of 18,000 and was distributed for free across Lenasia.

oppression and many of them worse oppression than South Africa," testified Allister Sparks.

"But South Africa is unique in one respect: It is the only country in the world that officially discriminated on the basis of race. Now, until the Second World War that was not uncommon. Since the Second World War and its powerfully symbolic exposure of the kind of excesses that could lead to, there has been a massive retreat over most of the globe from that. At the very time that retreat took place, South Africa moved more strongly than ever with the entrenchment of apartheid, the new philosophy that it had evolved in the course of the 1930s and which was applied then with great vigor and has been applied ever since and is still being applied.

"The effect of that is a very particular kind of oppression and it is a particular kind of oppression that is being reinforced in a number of ways by the press censorship being practiced in South Africa."

102.

A STATE OF EMERGENCY
(Open letter to P.W. Botha: June 1986)

a typed draft.

Mr. State President—

In this country torn apart by violence your white minority regime and its agents (my God, do you realize that in one line I have used three phrases described by the emergency regulations in South Africa!) have, through their arrogance, intransigence and organized campaigns of terror against the oppressed, created the circumstances you required for the declaration of a State of Emergency.

Annoyed, no doubt, by the courts, by interference from concerned bodies and individuals, parliamentary investigators, enterprising journalists and others who persisted to bring to light the truthe about your embattled regime, you have now succeeded in establishing a deadly silence surrounding yourselves: now no-one can report on what you are planning or doing, no-one can expose your lies and evils, no-one can speak up for those oppressed, hounded, turned out of their burning homes, tortured or killed by the latest incarnations of the Gestapo. Not even the names of those who are "disappearing" around us daily may be divulged.

103.

"The power of the media lies not only in their ability to reflect the dominant racial ideology, but in their capacity to define it in the first place."

—Michael Omi and Howard Winant

104.

A large white square dominated the front page of Wednesday's *Sowetan*. June 16, 1986. For the second consecutive day, the newspaper left its editorial column blank, except for a note saying any comment it could contribute "has been effectively banned."

In the *Johannesburg Star*, a similar absence: "Something happened at the University of the Witwatersrand residence in Soweto in the early hours of Sunday morning." Followed by a long blank space, and, "A spokesman for the Wits administration said those students who were unable to write their exams because they were in detention would be able to do so at a later date."

Journalists who violated emergency regulations were subject to jail terms of up to ten years or a fine up to twenty thousand rand.

105.

The President of the United States called the media the "enemy of the American people" for the first time.[42] February 17, 2017.

---

[42]This would not be the last.

106.

Jarrod Ramos barricaded the back door of the *Capital Gazette*'s newsroom before he started shooting. It was June 28, 2018. He killed five staffers, wounded two.[43]

John McNamara.
Wendi Winters.
Gerald Fischman.
Rob Hiaasen.
Rebecca Smith.

Surviving members of the newsroom reported out the day's news and published the next day's paper. The editorial page remained blank.

107.

Emergency regulations instituted by the Apartheid government in 1986 prohibited journalists "from being on

---

[43]And injured so many. Journalists hiding under their desks. The intern. Those working in the field or from home that day. For the first time, the US Freedom Tracker added a "killed" tag to the incident database. In 2018, the tracker documented more than one hundred press freedom incidents in twelve months. Five government employees were charged with allegedly leaking documents to the press, and eleven journalists were arrested doing their jobs.

the scene or within sight of any unrest, restricted gathering, or security action."

Within twelve months, twenty-six thousand South Africans were detained.

108.

When *New York Times* reporters reached South African journalists and political figures by phone during the State of Emergency, many declined to speak. They feared wiretapping and the repercussions of communicating under the new umbrella of restrictions.

"What the Bureau for Information tell us," said Percy Qoboza, editor of *City Press,* "has little resemblance to what we see with our own eyes, but we are prohibited by law from reporting it."

Another said he'd heard about the petrol-bombing of a church in Soweto, but confirmation was impossible with the new restrictions.

109.

President Botha issued the strictest press restrictions in South African history on December 11th, 1986. He warned of the country's "revolutionary onslaught," and that media controls needed "pepping up." Moving forward, any news or comment on the following topics were forbidden:

(1) security force actions;

(2) details of any planned "restricted gathering" or remarks made at such a gathering;

(3) the success of boycotts or any pressures exerted to enforce the boycotts;

(4) the operations of unlawful local political structures (such as street committees and "people's courts");

(5) remarks by persons under government restriction orders if the remarks are thought to endanger public order; and

(6) the circumstances or treatment of detainees.

The following year would be one of the country's worst for press freedom, banned media, and detaining journalists.

January 8, 1987—Police Commissioner Johan Coetzee issues restrictions forbidding newspapers from publishing reports or advertisements deemed to further the cause of "unlawful organizations." The ban is apparently aimed at the African National Congress: the previous day several newspapers published United Democratic Front advertisements calling for the legalization of the ANC.

February 20, 1987—Two alternative publications, the student newspaper *Saspu National* and the *Free Azania*, are ordered to submit the contents of all future issues to a publications control board for prior censorship. The requirement sets these publications apart from the rest of the press, which is required to seek authorization only for articles that may be problematic in terms of the regulations.

February 21, 1987—Graham Brown, a South African reporter for Agence France-Presse, arrested in the "tribal homeland" of Transkei while trying to cover the aftermath of a coup attempt in the neighboring homeland of Ciskei. Brown is released two days later.

Mid-March, 1987—Two issues of the black-run, Catholic-funded *New Nation* newspaper are banned by a publications control board, although they have been circulating since February. Zwelakhe Sisulu, editor of the *New Nation*, has been imprisoned since December 12.

May 13, 1987—*Sunday Star* reporter Jon Qwelane, photographer Herbert Mabuza, and their driver are detained in the homeland of KwaNdebele. They intended to cover the unrest in the homeland related to the issue of accepting independence from South Africa. Instead, they end up doing a story about the brutality against detainees they witnessed during their three-day detention in a police cell.

June 1987—*Eastern Province Herald* editor-in-chief Koos Viviers and former *Herald* reporter Jo-Ann Bekker are convicted under the Police Act for publishing untruths about the police in a 1985 article on unrest in Cradock. Viviers was fined one hundred rand and suspended for a year, and

Bekker was fined two hundred rand or one month in jail, and suspended for three years.

August 28, 1987—The July 30 and August 16 editions of the progressive Western Cape weekly newspaper *South*, the August issue of the far-right publication *Die Stem*, and an August issue of the black-run, Catholic Church-supported *New Nation* are banned under the Publications Act for containing "undesirable" material.

September 8, 1987—Marimuthu Subramoney, managing editor of the Press Trust of South Africa in Durban, is refused a passport.

September 1987—Police stop *Weekly Mail* reporter Mono Badela at a roadblock on his way to Port Elizabeth, search his car, and find copies of the *Weekly Mail* in the trunk. He is detained for about six hours and questioned about his work and colleagues. Badela has applied several times for a passport but has never been given one.

September 1987—The *Weekly Mail* is informed that it is under investigation for two possible contraventions of the emergency regulations: running an advertisement from the End Conscription Campaign in June 1987, and a February 1987 article on psychiatric treatment administered to a detainee. Johannesburg's *City Press* is also being investigated for its coverage of police removing a barbed wire fence that had been erected around Port Elizabeth, an issue which the police claim was a security matter.

October 2, 1987—The *New Nation* receives a written warning from the Home Minister that recent issues pose "a threat to the maintenance of public order." The warning is the first application of new emergency powers assumed by the Minister on August 28.

November 20, 1987—Authorities inform David C. Turnley of the *Detroit Free Press* that he must leave the country by November 30. He is accused of sending "biased photo material" overseas. Turnley is the thirteenth foreign journalist to be expelled from South Africa since the state of emergency was declared in June 1986.

110.

In the summer of 2020, there were 291 reported incidents with journalists covering George Floyd protests. In the lead up to and month after the presidential elections, eighty-one incidents were reported with journalists covering related protests. Through the entirety of 2020, journalists reported 698 press freedom violations and incidents with authorities when covering Black Lives Matter protests.

111.

Four days before parliamentary elections in 1989, thousands from the Mass Democratic Movement gathered to march in Cape Town in protest of the nation's exclusion of twenty-six million Black South Africans from the election process—part of a month-long defiance campaign. The plan: peacefully walk through the city and end at Parliament.

The South African Police emerged in Green Market square with a water cannon vehicle. The goal: break up the crowds, then follow-up with arrests. As they opened the cannon's nozzle, a jet of purple water shot into the crowd, against the walls of white buildings, breaking windows and staining everything in its path. A protestor climbed on top of the cannon, moved the hose away from protestors, and directed the purple spray toward the white National Ruling Party's headquarters. The police tear gassed the crowd.

Purple people dispersed throughout the city. Fifty-two journalists were arrested that day.

Days later, a nearby building was tagged "The Purple Shall Govern."

112.

Simon Nkoli organized the Saturday Group in Soweto, encouraging Black membership in GASA and intersectional and mixed-race socializing and discussion. Simon was an activist. He'd marched in the student uprisings in 1976 and was detained for several months during high school. He came out to his family and friends in 1978. He was an openly gay political activist within the Congress of South African Students and the United Democratic Front, and was an early member of GASA.

Simon attended GASA gatherings, was an active organizer, and was pictured in an issue of *Link/Skeykl* standing between two white men, both of whom he'd beaten in a GASA sporting event. Simon's face is featureless. The photograph is exposed for the white faces beside him. Simon's presence in the paper was noticed.

The anti-Apartheid movement was boiling with boycotts, marches, and violence. Simon helped organize the rent boycott demonstration in Sebokeng township. He was arrested and held in custody for nine months. Along with twenty-one others, Simon was charged with treason, sedition, and incitement to murder. The Delmas 22.

A letter writing campaign, including international LGBT organizations, supported Simon as he awaited trial. But the Gay Association of South Africa stayed silent. They saw themselves as apolitical. Simon saw his Blackness and his gayness as equally political in South Africa.

He would stay in prison for more than two years awaiting trial. He wrote letters to his love, Roy Shepherd. The two corresponded about GASA, their dreams, the movements, feelings of abandonment, and the idea of allyship. Simon read and he listened to music. James Baldwin, Franz Kafka, Danielle Steel. Marilyn French. Peter Tosh, Grace Jones, Gladys Knight and the Pips.

In South Africa's longest trial, Simon was acquitted.

Within months of his release, Simon formed GLOW—Gay and Lesbian Organization of Witswaterand. Chapters formed in Hillbrow, Berea, Soweto, Yeoville, and KwaThema,[44] in unassuming places like the home of Thokozile Khumalo. A heterosexual woman, MaThoko had opened her home on Legodi Street to gay, lesbian, and trans teens for more than a decade. Simon's identity and activism were inextricably linked—the anti-Apartheid movement and gay liberation represented his whole experience. And, so, GLOW would do the same.

With it came the *Glowletter*, a monthly with organizational updates, advertisements for pen pals, international gay rights news, book reviews, comics, and letters from GLOW members speaking to the formation of a new media group, a lesbian forum, and the AIDS working group led by Simon.

The *Glowletter* had visibility and reach. It was inside Phambili Books and the Johannesburg library. It was found in allied bookstores and community spaces. And its pages were used to not only build a coalition and inform, but it is also where GLOW protested against the lack of confidentiality in HIV cases and campaigned for the inclusion of a gay and lesbian rights charter within the country's new constitution. And many of the most controversial or nuanced subjects they tackled were most successful in full-page nonfiction comics, bringing text and image together to teach and connect.

---

[44]Named after Thema Selope.

Its reach is evident in pen pal listings—Ghana, Ukraine, US, Norway—and letters from teens in rural communities struggling to find a space where a group of young queer kids can meet in their community.

113.

The Truth and Reconciliation Commission included the press. It addressed issues of censorship, banning, race, gender, prison time, spies in the newsroom, and violence. Alternative papers participated. Black papers participated. Township papers participated. English-language press participated. "The Afrikaans press declined to make a submission to the Commission. Instead, it provided the Commission with a copy of "Oor Grense Heen," the official history of Nasionale Pers (Naspers)."

114.

In 2018, reporter and West Virginia native Molly Born moved to Williamson in the heart of the state's southern coalfields. From her apartment above an old dry cleaners on a quiet main street, she sought to cover communities that had long lacked representation in the state's newspapers and on the public radio station. Molly moved there to report for West Virginia Public Broadcasting, leaving a higher-paying position at the *Pittsburgh Post-Gazette.* She had to navigate deep-seated distrust from residents across the region she covered who couldn't believe that a reporter would come to live in their town at all.

Just north of her, Caity Coyne joined the *Charleston Gazette-Mail* with the same beat—address the long-standing coverage gap of the southern coal fields. The newsroom had won the Pulitzer Prize for investigative reporting one year earlier and featured several powerhouse reporters, including Ken Ward, who would be named a MacArthur Genius Fellow that same year. To the west, Will Wright moved into a trailer down by a creek in eastern Kentucky with the aim of reopening the long-closed Pikeville bureau for the *Lexington Herald-Leader.* He became a bureau of one covering thirteen rural counties.

Quickly, Will learned residents of southeastern Kentucky did not trust the *Lexington Herald-Leader.* They saw journalists as outsiders and, historically speaking, they are correct—most journalists parachute into regions like this to report a story and depart when they think they have it. They believed journalists did little more than perpetuate stereotypes. That journalists write stories about them, not for them.

Within his first few weeks there, Will attended a meeting that revealed a significant water crisis for residents in Martin County. The intake pump connected to the district's treatment plant had shut down due to freezing winter weather. They had a spare pump, but the district was $800,000 in debt and had no cash flow to make the necessary repairs. So, they shut off the water, hoping for the natural water pressure to sort things out.

Residents were angry.

Will covered the issue closely and regularly.

His reporting put pressure on the troubled general manager of the water district, who subsequently retired, and prompted then-Kentucky Governor Matt Bevin and US Senator Hal Rogers to quickly promise $4.6 million in federal grants to help address the crumbling infrastructure. The district also approved a rate hike that would begin to chip away at their debt.

This all happened within the first few months of the year. And because of this, Will was eventually met with "far more hospitality than distrust or resentment" as he reported on issues that mattered most to the region.

But, while Will Wright was reporting on the water issue, Caity Coyne was only weeks into starting at the *Charleston Gazette-Mail* when it declared bankruptcy. The paper went up for auction, secured new local owners, and then started layoffs.

The *Gazette-Mail* was not out of the woods. Like all papers in America, they'd been hit hard by advertising and subscription losses. Nationally, in 1990, more than sixty-two million households subscribed to newspapers. In 2018, that number was less than half that. Between 2004 and 2018, one in five papers shuttered, and closures are not slowing anytime soon.

115.

The *Villager*'s newsroom was tucked between the railroad tracks and Anjo's Chicken and Car Wash in Acornhoek, South Africa. Every time the train passed, travelling along the line that once divided the Lebowa and Gazankulu homelands, a plume of dust and trash would make its way into the newsroom through a large hole in the tin roof. One of the five journalists on staff—Linky Matsie, Thandi Mkhatshwa, Bongekile Mhlanga, Cosi Rahlane, and Thandy Ndlovu—would stand from their desk, sweep the cement floor from the west to the east, out the back door with the chickens or the goat, and then return to their drafting or edits.

In 2008, the monthly paper printed 7,500 copies. Based on issues being read to families and neighbors and the number of times it would pass from one hand to the next, the *Villager*'s purchase-to-toilet-paper-readership was estimated at sixty thousand. The all-women Shangaan and Northern Sotho staff covered the peri-urban community they called home—Acornhoek, Mpumalanga.

That year, the *Villager* covered the Bushbuckridge mayor's arrest for double murder, the safety of local creches, the conflict around the right to bury Sinois Masangwane Mokoena in Welverdiend, a local butchery supervisor stabbing his ex-girlfriend after a lunchtime quarrel, and a program serving seventy-five orphaned children in Thulamahashe. They covered the rise of carjackings, a local marula festival, a farm worker killed by a hippo, the presidential elections after Mbeki's resignation, and load-shedding. They wrote profiles of community members, covered school sports, and investigated local concerns like the rise in school fees and the correlation between the proximity of shebeens to schools and teen alcoholism—a story that would win Linky the region's Vodacom Community Journalist of the Year Award.

Lydia Ngomane sold the *Villager*'s advertising. After the distribution of each issue, she would walk her way along the main drag of Acornhoek selling classifieds. Where an outdoor butchery occupied an old petrol station and a funeral parlor was situated in the attached garage. Where an AIDS education center sat across the street from a West African doctor selling cures for the pandemic that, at the time, was predicted to kill forty percent of the local youth population throughout the aughts. Where BMWs were parked outside crumbling cement homes and the availability of water changed with the day of the week. Flyers screaming "Jesus saves and Heals!" wallpapered cell phone towers, and a sign to the province's largest hospital—just across the railroad tracks—had been hand-painted on corrugated tin.

Lydia sold lines in the business directory for five rand and classifieds for twenty-five. Fridah Hair Salon. Loa Hotel. Mpapele Music Production. Acu's Tent Hire and Deco. Rise and Shine Tuck Shop. Pink's Hair Salon. Teddy Bear Day Care. Chicken Lickin. Kenrodg Driving School.

Before the *Villager,* the papers sold along this same stretch of road came from Jo'burg—a five-hour drive to the west—or Nelspruit—two hours to the south. The *Sun.* The *Star.* The *Sowetan.* The *Lowvelder.* All news from far away.

116.

In January 2019, the *Orlando Sentinel* asked its readers for absolution, just days before Florida's Governor accepted the State Legislature's recommendation to formally apologize to four Black men accused of raping a young white woman seventy years earlier.

Three of the accused were arrested in 1949. Samuel Shepherd, Walter Irvin, and Charles Greenlee. A cartoon on the front page of the *Sentinel* then depicted four empty electric chairs with the caption, "No Compromise!" Within days the fourth accused, Ernest Thomas was shot by a group of men in a manhunt. Similar mobs started to burn the homes of Black residents.

"The story had many more ugly twists and turns marked by lies, cover-ups and injustice. You wouldn't know it from reading the *Orlando [Morning] Sentinel* in the years immediately following the incident," the editorial board confessed.

The *Sentinel*'s coverage tainted the ability for a fair trial in the local courts. This fact was even cited in the 1951 Supreme

Court decision overturning the convictions of Shepherd and Irvin based on the unconstitutional exclusion of Black residents from the jury.

Later in 1949, Shepherd and Irvin were being transported from prison to jail by the Lake County Sheriff when both men were shot on an isolated backroad. The only witness was the sheriff who shot them, claiming they were trying to escape. Shepherd died. Irvin survived and claimed the sheriff had instructed them to get out of the vehicle and then tried to assassinate them.

Soon after, the *Sentinel* published an editorial in absolute support of the sheriff, asserting, "we have no doubt he was telling the truth" about shooting in self-defense.

Twenty-one years after that incident, the sheriff that killed Shepherd would be removed from office as he was indicted for the murder of another Black prisoner.

Irvin was retried and imprisoned until his release in 1968. Greenlee was released in 1962. But, in 2012, after all four men had passed, an FBI investigation revealed that the 1949 medical examinations of their accuser showed no evidence of an assault. It would take another seven years for the newspaper to admit its role in the men's convictions.

"Today," the *Sentinel*'s editorial closes, "we ask the public's pardon for a period when our coverage fell short."

The *Sentinel* was not the first newspaper to admit guilt.

In 2000, the *Jackson Sun* in Tennessee published a series of articles on the civil rights movement and created an online resource that chronicled events throughout Jackson in the 1950s and 60s—an attempt to cover today what wasn't covered then.

In 2004, the *Lexington Herald-Leader* in Kentucky apologized for its failure to adequately cover the civil rights movement. At the time that the movement was changing the country, the newspaper's management operated under the principle that the less coverage they gave the movement, the quicker it would go away. Until the 2004 apology and the special insert published alongside it, images and reportage about protests in Lexington and sit-ins across the city had rarely, if ever, been published by the city's local paper.

In 2006, the *Charlotte Observer* and the *News & Observer* in North Carolina both apologized for their roles in the Wilmington Race Riots of 1898. "We apologize to the black citizens and their descendants whose rights and interests we disregarded," the *Observer* wrote, "and to all North Carolinians, whose trust we betrayed by our failure to fairly report the news and stand firm against injustice." Each paper's editorial ran alongside a jointly produced sixteen-page special report titled, "A Painful Past," chronicling events that led to the riots and anti-Black activities, including efforts by local newspapers to support white supremacists and seek the removal of anti-segregationists from office.

Just two days before Obama's inauguration in 2008, the *Meridian Star*, a daily paper that covers eastern Mississippi and western Alabama, apologized for its past coverage of civil rights issues.

117.

Crystal Good printed and distributed the first issue of *Black by God* in 2020. Five thousand copies were dropped off in total, a bundle here and a bundle there, making its way through West Virginia to this person's porch and that person's porch, who would then bring copies to their coffee shop or church or pharmacy in town. This "mutual aid network" allowed Crystal to see possibility.

When Crystal Good was fifteen, the *Beacon Digest* was the only Black paper in West Virginia. For the most part, it was the only Black paper in the state from its launch in 1956 to its close fifty years later. Like so many small papers, the *Digest* had become a patchwork of AP stories and little else. Crystal knew she could do better. She wanted to purchase the paper. She didn't know how exactly, but her dad approached the owners, the Starks family, and tried to broker the deal for her. The owners declined, leaving Crystal to continue the cut and paste newspaper work she did for the high school. But she still held onto her dream to own a newspaper.

Black by God[45] is now the only Black newspaper in West Virginia. "It talks back," says Crystal. "It says: Yo, we're here. We've been here. We have something to say."

But Afrilachian poet and newspaper editor Crystal—a sixth generation West Virginian—knows she's up against a media landscape with more money and resources and staff reporters. For now, she is focused on building and reaching her audience.

With each issue, Crystal continues the grassroots approach to distribution. She piles a thousand pounds of papers in the back of her car and starts driving.

118.

Half of the 3,140 counties in the United States have only one paper, often a resource-stripped weekly paper, leaving enormous community and issue-based coverage gaps. More than two hundred counties have lost a news source entirely. In the span of ten years, newsroom employees across the country have been cut in half.

---

[45]The name *Black by God* comes from an early way folks differentiated West Virginia from Virginia, a division that took place in 1863, when they mentioned their state, "Black, by God, West Virginia". But Crystal points to how a woman by the name of Ada Beatrice Queen Victoria Smith— known as Brick Top—would always claim that she was from "West, by God, Virginia." In 1920, Brick Top made sure her story was in all the papers across America even though she was in Paris. And within each, they would always say she was from "West, by God, Virginia".

119.

Free newspapers across South Africa have retained their circulation. But the bulk of papers sold to readers saw a steep decline in circulation in the ten years before the pandemic. The *Sunday Times*, down seventy-five percent. The *Daily Sun,* down eighty-nine percent. The *Saturday Star*, down ninety-one percent.

The Covid-19 shut-downs only accelerated the loss of subscribers and readers. Print was too slow for the rapid-paced information South Africans were seeking about infection rates in their communities, testing sites, and the rules around movement between provinces. With electricity rates, load-shedding, and unemployment on the rise, free online news and texting services won out over printed newspapers sold in shops and on street corners.

Despite this, the digital-only, long form investigative news organization, the *Daily Maverick* wanted to launch a weekly newspaper. Print. As other newsrooms shrank, they grew—from a startup of five to a newsroom of more than one hundred. And, so, they continued with their willingness to try and possibly fail. They'd sought media partners with no bites. So, they sought a partner of another kind: the nation's largest grocery store.

In September 2020, they launched *168*, named for the hours in a single week, "a weekly paper for cool minds and fiery hearts".

120.

The annual World Press Freedoms Index is an in-depth analysis of the legal framework, political context, economic context, sociocultural context, and safety in 180 countries. Within the latter, confirmed reports of bodily harm, emotional distress, and professional harm are considered.

"After a sharp rise in 2020, freedom of the press violations have fallen significantly in the United States, but major structural barriers to press freedom persist in this country once considered a model for freedom of expression."

In 2023, South Africa was ranked twenty-fifth and the United States forty-fifth.

ACKNOWLEDGMENTS

So many individuals and institutions supported me and helped usher this book from pitch to reportage and publication. Only a few can be named here. A huge thanks to Christopher Schaberg, Ian Bogost, and Haaris Naqvi for seeing the potential in my unusual approach to chronicling the hidden lives behind newspapers and, even more, for their patience as I drafted and redrafted. The level of travel necessary to sit inside physical archives and libraries or to complete interviews in person was only possible because of a generous summer research grant provided by the Donald P. Bellisario College of Communications at the Pennsylvania State University, where I teach and direct the News Lab.

I have bottomless gratitude for my partner Kevin Haworth who joined me on the road for more than 2,600 km, zig-zagging my way across South Africa, to read through newspapers from as far back as Kimberley's diamond rush and to think about the four-hundred-year history of newspapers and press freedom in the two nations I call home. Even more, for his support whenever I disappear into my writing.

Lastly, this book is dedicated to my mother and the women journalists of Amazwi.

A NOTE ON SOURCES

This work took me inside digital and physical institutions—libraries, archives, newsrooms, and museums—in the United States and South Africa. Important sources of original newspapers, cited throughout this book, include the Africana Library in Kimberley, the National Library of South Africa in Cape Town, the Library of Congress in Washington DC, and the online collections of Digital Innovation South Africa and the Wisconsin Historical Society, among others.

What follows is only a select (and very short) list of sources used in the writing of this book. A comprehensive list, including an annotated bibliography of interviews, scholarly articles, original newspapers, podcasts, speeches, and books, is available on my website (maggiemessitt.com).

—

Akhalwaya, Ameen. "Through the Loopholes." *Index on Censorship* 17 no. 3 (1988): 24–26.

Adorno, Theodor. *Minima Moralia: Reflections from Damaged Life*, translated by E.F.N. Jephcott. London: Verso, 1978.

Barnard, Anne Lindsay. *South Africa a Century Ago; Letters Written from the Cape of Good Hope (1797–1801)*. London: Smith, Edler & Co, 1910.

Bell, Alexandra. "Art that Forms New Narratives," National Geographic Storytellers Summit. May 2019.

Berger, Dan and Toussaint Losier. "Revolution: The Prison Rebellion Years 1968–1972." In *Rethinking the American Prison Movement*. New York: Routledge, 2017.

Campion, Susan. "Wallpaper Newspapers of the American Civil War." *Journal of the American Institute for Conservation* Vol. 34, no. 2 (1995): 129–40.

Cheadle, Brian. "South African Serial Publications of the Anglo-Boer War." *Victorian Periodicals Review* Vol. 37, no. 4 (2004): 25–45.

Chimutengwende, Chenhamo C. "The Media and the State in South African Politics," *The Black Scholar* Vol. 10, no. 1 (1978): 44–57.

DiSalvo, Charles R. M.K. Gandhi, *Attorney at Law: The Man before the Mahatma*. Berkeley: University of California Press, 2013.

DuBois, W.E.B. "The Value of Agitation." *Voices of the Negro*, Vol. IV (March 1907): 109–110.

Everett, Christopher. *Wilmington on Fire*. Wilmington: Blackhouse Publishing, 2015.

First, Ruth. *117 Days*. New York: Monthly Review Press, 1989.

Goings, K. W., & G. L. Smith, "'Unhidden' Transcripts: Memphis and African American Agency, 1862-1920." *Journal of Urban History*, Vol. 21, no. 3 (1995): 372–394.

Harris, Jr., Roy. *Pulitzer's Gold: A Century of Public Service Journalism*. New York: Columbia University Press, 2015.

Harvey, Gail. *Human Rights Violations in Apartheid South Africa*. The Africa Fund (Sept 1983).

Harvey, Ira. *The Smell of Burning Crosses*. Jackson: University Press of Mississippi, 1967.

"History of the Queer Press," *Library Talks*, New York Public Library. June 2, 2019.

Hoe, Robert. *A Short History of the Printing Press* .New York: Robert Hoe Press,1902.

Klimonoff, Hank. "A Reporter who Refused to Run," *Media Studies Journal*, Vol. 14 no.2 (Spring/Summer 2000).

MacKellar, Thomas. *American Printer: A Manual of Typography*. Philadelphia: Mackellar, Smiths & Jordan, 1885.

Mayet, Juby. *Freedom Writers: My life and times*. Johannesburg: Jacana Media, 2022.

McMurtie, Douglas C. "The Printing Press Moves Westward." *Minnesota History: A Quarterly Magazine*, Vol. 15 no. 1. (1934).

"Media Restrictions in South Africa." Hearings before the Committee on Foreign Affairs, subcommittee on Africa, 100th Congress (March 15 & 16, 1988).

Ndzamela, Phakamisa. *Native Merchants: The Building of the Black Business Class in South Africa*. Cape Town: Tafelberg, 2021.

Paltsits, Victor. "New Light on *Public Occurrences*: America's First Newspaper," American Antiquarian Society (1949): 75–88.

Parsons, David L. *Dangerous Grounds: Antiwar Coffeehouses and Military Dissent in the Vietnam Era*. Chapel Hill: University of North Carolina Press, 2017.

Roudané, Mark Charles. "Grappling with the Memory of New Orleans." *The Atlantic*. (October 25, 2015).

Stephen Daye and his Successors: 1639–1921. Cambridge: University Press, 1921.

The Truth and Reconciliation Commission. *"Chapter 6: The Media," The Truth and Reconciliation Final Report*, Vol 4. (October 1998).

Tucker, David M. "Miss Ida B. Wells and Memphis Lynching." *Phylon (1960-)* Vol. 32, no. 2 (1971): 112–22.

"Wallpaper news of the sixties," National Park Service Popular Series. Washington: US Dept of the Interior, Government Printing Office, 1941.

INDEX